The FRIENDSHIP BOOK

of Francis Gay

D. C. THOMSON & CO., LTD.
London Glasgow Manchester Dundee
ISBN 0 85116 407 2

A Thought
For Each Day
In 1988

*A friend may well be reckoned
the masterpiece of Nature.*

SOLITUDE

Happy the man who finds his peace
At the end of the day when labours cease;
Contented to watch as that greater hand
Gilds His canvas of sea and land.

JANUARY

FRIDAY—JANUARY 1.

IT is almost inevitable, as we stand at the beginning of a New Year, that we should wonder what the future has in store for us. Some people face that unknown future with fear and foreboding. Yet how greatly that fear could be reduced if we remembered the words of an unknown writer who said, reassuringly, "The best thing about the future is that it comes one day at a time".

To learn to live a day at a time is one of the deepest secrets of serenity. As Jesus, said, "Sufficient unto the day is the evil thereof".

SATURDAY—JANUARY 2.

WE had enjoyed a lovely meal at our friend's house. I had particularly liked the fruit pudding, and I said so.

Maureen laughed. "I'll let you into a secret. That fruit pudding started life as a cake, but somebody came to the door when it was in the oven and it didn't turn out quite as I had intended."

"Well, it made a lovely pudding," I said, "so your cake wasn't wasted."

"I'm glad," said Maureen. "Long ago I got a tip from an old lady who had been a cook in a big house. She said to me: 'The golden rule in cooking is knowing how to retrieve your disasters.' It's something I've never forgotten."

I think Maureen's "golden rule" applies to more than cooking. I'm sure we can all think of men and women who have done great things after making a bad start in life.

THE FRIENDSHIP BOOK

SUNDAY—JANUARY 3.

PRAISE ye the Lord for it is good to sing praises unto our God.

Psalms 147:1

MONDAY—JANUARY 4.

OUR friend Mary's face lit up the other afternoon when the Lady of the House and I dropped in.

"Oh, I'm specially glad to see you today," she said. She went to the cupboard and brought out an unopened box of chocolates. "These were given to me last week and I've been waiting for someone to share them with. I enjoy them so much more that way!"

Happiness *is* sharing, isn't it? As the poet Conrad Aiken put it:

Music I heard with you was more than music,
And bread I broke with you was more than bread.

TUESDAY—JANUARY 5.

JAMES HERRIOT, author of the famous vet books, "All Creatures Great and Small", "It Shouldn't Happen to a Vet", and many others, has told how an old Yorkshire farmer said to him once in his local dialect, "Your books are all about nowt!"

Herriot comments, "I suppose he had a point because there is nothing world-shaking about my books — they are merely the chronicles of the little triumphs and disasters, the struggles and daily incidents of a veterinary surgeon's life."

In a sense, most of our lives could be said to be "all about nothing", and while we may not be able to present them in the humorous and fascinating way James Herriot does, at least it reminds us that an uneventful life need not be a dull one!

THE FRIENDSHIP BOOK

PATRICIA McGAVOCK of Belfast wrote this charming poem, "Life's Pattern":

> Oh, what a pattern we can weave
>   In three score years and ten!
> And not one thread can we unpick,
>   Or weave it in again;
> The threads of happy childhood,
>   Days filled with fun and joy;
> Excitements, pleasures, ecstasy
>   Of love when girl meets boy;
> The knot within the pattern
>   When promises are made
> To have, to hold, to cherish
>   With love that will not fade;
> The golden threads of friendship
>   We find along life's way,
> The happiness that we can share
>   With others day by day;
> Kind memory stores these threads for us,
>   That we might live again
> The golden days, when we have spanned
>   The three score years and ten.

SYDNEY SMITH, the clergyman, writer and wit, was said to have had four bedrooms which he used in turn during the four seasons of the year. His quarterly change of room reminded him of the changing seasons.

I remember a prayer in church in which the preacher gave thanks for "the changing seasons with their varied gifts of use and loveliness." Not a bad idea at the beginning of each new season to remember its particular blessings and beauties.

CONCENTRATION

THE FRIENDSHIP BOOK

HAVE you noticed how everything seems to be instant? Instant entertainment at the press of a button, instant information from computers, instant arithmetic from calculators, even instant potatoes! There's a danger, of course, that we come to expect everything to be instant — instant happiness and instant success.

The most important things in life are those which grow and develop, like friendships and love and forgiveness. These are seldom instant.

I once read this advice in a driving school prospectus: "If at first you don't succeed, remember you're running about average!"

That's not just good advice for learner drivers who are taking their test, it's good advice for all of us as we journey through life.

A TEACHER friend of ours had been talking to his class about what are known as the Seven Wonders of the World — the Pyramids of Egypt, the Hanging Gardens of Babylon, the Temple of Diana at Ephesus and so on.

Towards the end of the lesson, the teacher asked his pupils to compile a list of what they considered to be the Seven Wonders of the modern world, for technology has given us some pretty amazing things.

After they had been writing for some time, one of the boys raised his hand and said, "But please, sir, we can't do *just* seven, can we?"

How right he was! Our modern world is *full* of wonders. If you are feeling a bit depressed some time, it might not be a bad idea to make your own list — and you don't have to confine it to seven!

THE FRIENDSHIP BOOK

ASPIRE to lead a quiet life, to mind your own business, and to work with your own hands.

I Thessalonians 4:11

DR CYRIL TOWLSON was the well-loved head-master of a famous Yorkshire public school — Woodhouse Grove, near Bradford. He was an accomplished musician and a prominent Methodist.

A philosopher and thinker, Towlson had a great teacher's ability to impart deep truths in a few well-chosen words. Witness these simple, effective verses, which were found among his papers after his death:

Isn't it strange that princes and kings
And clowns that caper in circus rings
And common folk like you and me
Are builders for eternity?

To each is given a bag of tools,
A shapeless mass and a book of rules,
And each must make e'er time be flown
A stumbling block or stepping stone.

LISA, aged five, and Peter, a year younger, were going into church for a wedding. As they sat down, Lisa whispered to Peter that he mustn't say a word. "We're not allowed to," she said.

"Who won't let me?" he asked.

His sister pointed to the couple who were greeting people at the door and answered: "See that man and woman — they're hushers!"

NO HURRY

True friends have always time to spare,
A word to pass, a thought to share.

A

THE FRIENDSHIP BOOK

YEARS ago when the hooters blared out their early morning message to the thousands of workers in a big electrical plant in Manchester, one man always stopped outside a jeweller's shop. It had a particularly fine clock in the window and by this he set his watch.

For months the owner of the shop watched the man, and one morning he came out and asked him why he was so interested in this particular clock.

"Well," he replied, "it's my job to see that the factory clock is kept accurate so that we know when to set off the hooters."

The jeweller laughed. "Would you believe it," he said, "and all that time I've been setting the clock by your hooters!"

"YOU must visit Mrs Oliver who lives in the little cottage at the end of the High Street. She'll make you very welcome. She doesn't have many mod cons, but she does have an automatic kettle".

This advice was given by a church warden to a newly-arrived vicar in a country parish. He made a point of visiting Mrs Oliver, and when he knocked on her door, she welcomed him with a smile. Inside, he noticed an old kettle coming to the boil on her gas cooker. The teapot was filled, and they enjoyed a cup of tea together and chatted about the life of the village.

When the vicar next met the church warden he thanked him for his advice. He had indeed found Mrs Oliver's welcome encouraging. "But," he said, "she used an old kettle. I didn't notice an automatic one."

The church warden smiled. "As soon as she hears a knock on the door she *automatically* puts the kettle on," he said quietly.

THE FRIENDSHIP BOOK

I LIKE to pick up shells from the beach and over the years I have made quite a collection.

In the Middle Ages many people went on pilgrimages and the emblem they wore on their journey was a scallop shell. It was chosen because it was the emblem of St. James of Compostela, in Spain, whose shrine attracted many pilgrims. The scallop shells found round the Spanish coast are bigger than any shells we find on our own beaches in Britain, so they came in useful on the journey as spoons, cups, or even dishes. It was the custom to keep your pilgrim shell stuck in your hat where it would be readily available.

The scallop shell is still used as an emblem for pilgrims today, and on the signs which mark the old Pilgrims' Way from Winchester to Canterbury, the shell can still be seen.

IT'S easy to feel sorry for someone . . . not so easy to do something useful to help. I'm thinking of two schoolgirls, Victoria and Joanne, who were going home in an Essex town, on a freezing night, when they saw an old lady wandering in the road, nearly blue with cold.

The two girls did a bit of quick thinking. They used a coat and their scarves, wrapped them round the old lady, and took her, confused and shivering, to a nearby hostel, very probably saving her life.

Nothing very wonderful, you may say, and I suppose it isn't. But I only hope if ever I'm in trouble I meet people like Joanne and Victoria and not someone, who is so very sorry but decides that there is really nothing he or she can do about it . . .

THE FRIENDSHIP BOOK

SUNDAY—JANUARY 17.

A FRIEND loves at all times.

Proverbs 17:17

MONDAY—JANUARY 18.

IT was a snowy morning in January and the minister did not expect a large congregation. Least of all did he expect Mrs Brown, a crippled woman in her eighties, to be there, but she was.

"However did you manage to make the journey on a day like this?" asked the minister as he welcomed her.

"Ah, well, my heart gets here first," she answered brightly. "After that, it's easy for the rest of me!"

True of more than church-going, isn't it?

TUESDAY—JANUARY 19.

LIZ was a successful secretary who had long said she wanted to paint. She bought the most expensive materials: fine canvas, oil paints, a good easel. Books by the dozen were borrowed from the library and read from cover to cover. Yet all her canvases remained blank: not one picture was completed.

Jean, on the other hand, had little money. She could afford only a few basic colours and oiled paper on which to apply them, but she persevered. Her pictures were primitive but much admired at exhibitions in the village hall. A few of them were purchased, thus providing her with money to buy more and better materials.

Jean knew what Liz had forgotten: that fortune favours the bold; success attends those who have the courage to try.

THE FRIENDSHIP BOOK

I DON'T know about you, but I'm very much saddened by all the notices appearing in stores these days: "Shoplifters will be prosecuted"; "This shop employs store detectives"; "Surveillance equipment in operation" etc.

I'm sorry that these are thought necessary, but appreciate, of course, that if the deterrents *do* prove effective, then our goods will presumably be less expensive in the long run.

I couldn't help smiling, though, when I saw a notice that could prove to be the ultimate deterrent. Prominently displayed in a Christian bookshop was the sign: "Shoplifters will be *prayed for*"!

THIS year marks the 50th anniversary of the posthumous publication of the diary of the Rev. Francis Kilvert who died in 1879. This modest, unworldly curate died at an early age after serving for seven years in the country parish of Clyro in Radnorshire. Here he endeared himself to his parishioners by his faithful ministry, walking miles over the hilly countryside to visit those in need and read the Bible to those who were unable to do it for themselves.

But it is his beautifully-kept diary which has made him known today, with its unique picture of life as a Victorian village clergyman. In it we have lovely cameos of the people he moved amongst — the landowners, labourers, the old, the children — and all linked together by his beautiful descriptions of the Black Mountains and the Welsh border country.

The cross on Kilvert's grave is inscribed with the words, "He being dead yet speaketh". A true epitaph.

ARTISTRY

A glorious canvas, never repeated;
Shades unknown to the palette of man.
Try though he will to capture the magic,
A minor artist, he never can.

THE FRIENDSHIP BOOK

TWO strangers once met under a signpost by a crossroads. One of them was a tramp.

"In your life of wandering," the other asked him, "how do you decide where to go each day?"

"Oh, I see which way the wind is blowing, make sure it is behind me, and that's the way I go," was the tramp's reply. And he put his statement into practice by stepping off in the same direction as the wind.

The other man watched him go, then looked at the signpost and set off in the opposite direction up a steep hill.

Some of us may envy that old tramp, but in life, would it really be pleasant always to take the easy way? There's a lot to be said, isn't there, for the burden of responsibility, the joy of a task well done, the satisfaction of a battle won.

THE other day the Lady of the House and I stopped to look in the window of a secondhand shop. On display were many domestic items which once had a place in every household.

"Oh, Francis," she said, "a lot of these are exactly the kind of things I threw away years ago! Just look at the price they're fetching now!"

I couldn't help feeling that there are other things, too, that people have "thrown out" without realising the value — moral standards which are considered old-fashioned, Sunday as a day of rest, the sanctity of marriage vows, the solidarity of family life, and much more besides.

Just because a thing is old it is not necessarily old-fashioned. There are old ideals and standards well worth keeping.

THE FRIENDSHIP BOOK

FOR I have given you an example, that you should do as I have done to you.   John 13:15

SIR THOMAS BEECHAM, the great English conductor, once said, "The English don't care much for music, but they do like the noise it makes!"

Well, Beecham was given to saying rather outrageous things, but I think there is an element of truth behind those words. We don't need to be trained musicians to enjoy music. We don't need to be skilled technicians to get pleasure from a motor car or a television set.

There's a lot in life that we may not be able to understand or explain, but if we can get happiness from it we should gratefully do so.

THERE is a delightful scene in the film "The King and I" when Deborah Kerr meets the King's many children — her future pupils — and quickly endears herself to them. She tells them of the ancient adage about teaching — in the end "By your pupils you'll be taught."

I thought about this recently when reading a note from a schoolteacher. She had been testing her young charges in General Knowledge.

"Tell me, John," she questioned one small boy, "Which month has 28 days?"

"Please, miss," came the quick response, "they all have!"

What could the poor teacher say? After all the lad was right!

THE FRIENDSHIP BOOK

I TRIED to call to mind today
A worry I had yesterday.
But what it was and why and how
I simply can't remember now!

WEDNESDAY—JANUARY 28.

IN the preface to her fascinating book, "Water in England", Dorothy Hartley writes, "Our water was always important. Before roads were built it was our travel guide and map-maker. We caught it running, kept it static, conducted it and made it work for us. We washed in it (homesick Romans built Bath for it); we even drank it sometimes. Our saints made it miraculous, minerals made it medical."

Water! How much we take it for granted! When next we turn the tap we might remember that bit of potted history above and also the millions in the world who suffer through prolonged drought and polluted water supplies. My prayer for today is, "Give us this day our daily water".

FRIDAY—JANUARY 29.

THERE is an old legend about a demon who was sent to tempt a holy man. He tried all his wiles, but none of them succeeded. At last, an older and more experienced demon said, "Let me try." He crept up behind the saintly man and whispered, "Your brother has just been made Bishop of Alexandria." Sad to relate, that did the trick!

Envy! If we can fight successfully against *that* and be content with what we have, sincere in our appreciation of others' good fortune, then we shall have gone a long way along the road to true happiness.

THE FRIENDSHIP BOOK

VERY often encouragement comes from words written or spoken by people who have known real trouble of one sort or another. John Bunyan's "Pilgrim's Progress", written in a 17th century jail, is an example.

On another occasion he wrote, "There is nothing like faith to help at a pinch; faith dissolves doubt as the sun drives away mist — let it rain, let it blow, let it thunder, let it lighten, a Christian must still believe."

During the terrible days of persecution, a young Jew wrote on the wall of his ghetto:

"I believe in the sun, even if it does not shine,
I believe in love, even if I do not feel it,
I believe in God, even if I do not see Him."

After the war, Group Captain Leonard Cheshire, war hero and founder of the country-wide Cheshire Homes, had many ups and downs when trying to discover the best way to use his life. In his "Autobiography and Reflections" he stated: "A spirit of adventure, of putting one's self and one's future second, and the needs of the deprived first, comes as a breath of fresh air."

Eventually this way of helping less fortunate people became his way of life, but he realised the help had to be given because of the persons themselves, not just because of their handicap. He wrote: "If I am physically disabled and dependent upon someone else's support, I have a special need to feel what is being done for me is not out of a sense of duty, or still worse pity, but purely because I am me."

SUNDAY—JANUARY 31.

AND come hither, and I shall light a candle of understanding in thine heart.   II Esdras 14:25

FEBRUARY

MONDAY—FEBRUARY 1.

A SMALL boy was asked, " What do you think God is like?" His reply was, " He isn't a ' think '; He's a feel '!"

Could a theologian give us any better answer?

TUESDAY—FEBRUARY 2.

FEBRUARY 2nd is Candlemas Day, known mainly nowadays because it is a Scottish Quarter Day, but in the Middle Ages it used to be an important church festival.

It commemorated the Purification of the Virgin Mary, and people gathered in their churches for the blessing of the candles and tapers which were to be used during the year. The lighted candles were then carried in procession round the church for it was believed that they would give protection against evil spirits.

Snowdrops are still known as Candlemas bells and an old rhyme, sung by a procession of girls in white dresses, goes:

The snowdrop in purest white array
First rears her head on Candlemas Day.

Candlemas, with the days lengthening, was regarded as the turning point of Winter and the prospect of Spring days to follow:

If Candlemas Day be fair and bright,
Winter will have another flight;
But if Candlemas Day be clouds and rain,
Winter is gone and will not come again.

THE FRIENDSHIP BOOK

WHEN a friend of mine retired recently, he enjoyed spending a little time each morning sitting with a friend on a seat which the council had put under a large oak tree. It was by a small green near the busy junction of two roads.

Later, in the local museum, my friend saw some photographs of the same green as it was 50 or more years ago. How things had changed, he thought. Then he noticed that the tree was there in all the photographs. It gave him a sense of wonder to think that the tree would still be there long after his life was ended.

Trees are our oldest living things. What a joy they are and what a variety of them we have! Did you know that in California there are trees 350 feet high — as high as the dome of St Paul's Cathedral in London? They are more than 3,000 years old. They must have been saplings when Abraham was alive!

THE late Ursula Bloom is perhaps best-known as a romantic novelist. She was authoress of several hundred books written under a variety of noms-de-plume as well as her own name.

In a way, she was a bit of a philosopher, too. I have often pondered a saying of hers, which on first sight may sound a bit extravagant. However, the more I think about it, the more I am convinced it is true.

"Never regret anything you have ever done," she wrote, "it was all experience. Even if you made rather a fool of yourself — well that was valuable experience, too. You are the richer for everything that has ever happened to you. That is a hard lesson to learn, but I am glad to have learned it."

CONTEMPLATION

There's time to daydream,
Time to think,
In a quiet spot
By the water's brink.

THE FRIENDSHIP BOOK

AT the beginning of the last century, anyone passing the ruins of Elgin Cathedral, in Moray, might have seen a rather eccentric-looking man busily clearing away rubbish.

John Shanks was a shoemaker, but he also had a talent for practical archaeology. Because of his interest, the local authorities decided in 1824 that he should be appointed Keeper of the Cathedral. So well was their faith justified that John Shanks devoted himself to the job for 25 years.

He never stopped working. He cleared all the accumulated rubbish in the nave that had lain there since 1711. With his own hands, he moved 3000 barrowloads of debris, rediscovering the foundations of the pillars, the elevation to the altar and the steps of the western entrance.

Yet with it all, John always had time to tell visitors about the Cathedral and its glorious past. No wonder Elgin still remembers John Shanks, an ordinary man who worked wonders.

WE are accustomed to kings and queens being enthroned at their coronations, for the throne is a symbol of power and authority. But in the ancient African kingdom of Ashanti, on what used to be called the Gold Coast, the king was not enthroned but "stooled", the lowly stool being the royal symbol, lowliness not loftiness being the quality which was expected of royalty.

How grateful we should be that still in our own communities there are men and women who, whilst given positions of authority, see it as their mission in life humbly to serve others. That's real "kingship".

THE FRIENDSHIP BOOK

LET your light so shine before men, that they may see your good works and glorify your Father.

Matthew 5:16

THE Lady of the House was collecting for the new minister due to be inducted soon. Most of the parishioners had given cheerfully enough with comments such as "I hope we like him" and "I hope he's a good visitor". Her last call was at the tiny home of an elderly widow. She knew there was very little money there, but the old lady would not want to be missed out.

As soon as she knocked on the door, a smiling face appeared. "You'll be collecting for the new minister," she said, and after donating a generous contribution added, "I do hope he likes us!"

PETER had been rehearsing for the Gang Show for weeks as a cub. Every new song that he learned was taught to his young brothers, and he regaled all the details of the sketches to his father who had been an invalid for some time. It was disappointing that Dad would be unable to watch the show, but he was kept in touch with progress after every rehearsal.

Then, two weeks before the first night, Peter's father died. All the children were plunged into a state of shock, and Peter missed a rehearsal. However, he turned up for the next one, saying, "Now Dad will be able to see the show. He'll have the best seat of all!"

And if ever anyone played to the gallery all the week of the Gang Show, it was young Peter.

THE FRIENDSHIP BOOK

THE writer of this poem is unknown to me, but what an example it sets:

I will start anew this morning with a higher, fairer creed;
I will cease to stand complaining of my ruthless neighbour's greed;
I will cease to sit repining while my duty's clear,
I will waste no moment whining, and my heart shall know no fear.
I will look sometimes about me for the things that merit praise;
I will search for hidden beauties that elude the grumbler's gaze;
I will try to find contentment in the paths that I must tread;
I will cease to have resentment when another moves ahead.
I will not be swayed by envy when my rival's strength is shown;
I will not deny his merit, but I'll strive to prove my own;
I will try to see the beauty spread before me, rain or shine;
I will cease to preach your duty and be more concerned with mine.

A SUCCESSFUL businessman once told his audience, " The most tactful man I ever knew is the one who fired me from my first job. He called me in and said, ' Son, I don't know how we're ever going to get on without you, but starting on Monday, we're going to try.' "

THE inventor, Thomas Edison, was once asked to define electricity. He replied, "It exists. Use it!"

There are lots of things which we may not understand, but which, if we use them, can bring us great benefits. I don't really understand much of what goes on under the bonnet of a motor car, but that does not stop me getting pleasure and convenience from its use.

Much the same may be said of radio or television. Few of us have the technical knowledge to understand these complicated pieces of apparatus and yet we derive enjoyment from them.

But it seems to me that the most complicated piece of apparatus of all is a human being! Ourselves! We are capable of so much if only we allow the Holy Spirit to guide us. It's all a great mystery, but, as Edison said, we don't have to explain it. All we have to do is use it.

A FRIEND of ours recently had trouble with her eyes. She found herself seeing double—a disturbing condition, but one which, fortunately, the eye specialist was able to correct.

I could not help remembering a rather startling remark made by the late Dr W. E. Sangster, the well-known Methodist preacher. He said, "Jesus sees double . . . " Then he went on to say, "He sees us not only as the people we are, but as the people we might become. 'Thou art Simon . . . thou shalt be Peter'."

Would that we all had this "double vision" about people, seeing the best in them. Such "seeing double" would help them and help us. Let's try it!

THE FRIENDSHIP BOOK

OPEN my eyes, that I may see wondrous things
from your law.   Psalms 119:18

IN her autobiography "Journey From the North",
Storm Jameson recalls the period of wartime
rationing and shortages. She tells how her writer
friend, Noel Streatfield, and her housekeeper, had
each been given an orange by their greengrocer and
they decided to give them to Storm, who had not had
one for at least two years.

As she left, Noel said, "They're small and probably
sour, but an orange is an orange."

Storm Jameson adds, "She was wrong on both
counts, They were not sour, and an orange is
sometimes a miracle."

A lovely story, not least because it reminds us that
by simple acts of kindness and generosity we can *all*
work miracles.

IN some countries, particularly in the East, old age
seems to be treated with a good deal more respect
than it is in our modern society.

In Japan, for example, there is a nationally-
observed Respect for Age Day, while in Thailand, life
is divided into cycles of 12 years. At the end of the
fifth cycle, at the age of 60, people are given, with very
great respect, the title of Grandfather or
Grandmother, while at the end of the next cycle they
are called Very Old Grandfather or Very Old
Grandmother.

Rather a lovely custom, don't you think!

THE FRIENDSHIP BOOK

OVER the years I have found our old friend Mary to be a pretty shrewd judge of character. She doesn't say a great deal, but what she says is very much to the point. We were talking about a mutual friend and I was both amused and impressed by the way she summed him up: "I like him," she said. "He's upright and he's downright — so, as far as I'm concerned, he's all right!"

ONE of my favourite chroniclers of village life is Mary Russell Mitford, who was born in 1787. From her gifted pen came the sketches which were eventually collected into book form, and published in many editions as "Our Village".

Mary was the daughter of an extravagant, gambling doctor and an ailing mother. They were very hard-up and her writing was the only means of survival for the household. Yet, towards the end of her life, worn out with years of literary effort, Mary could still write gratefully, "It has pleased Providence to preserve to me my calmness of mind, clearness of intellect, my cheerfulness and my enjoyment of little things. This very day, a saucy troop of sparrows have been pecking at their tray of breadcrumbs outside the window. How much delight there is in common objects, if people would but learn to enjoy them!"

Mary's ability to do just this, and to record life in her beloved Berkshire village of Three Mile Cross, was to give pleasure to countless readers. Vitally aware of all that went on around her, Mary continued her efforts until her arthritic joints could hardly hold a pen. But she had saved her family from destitution; her life's work had been a true labour of love.

THE FRIENDSHIP BOOK

CHRISSY GREENSLADE here expresses her thoughts about birthdays and tells us why we should be grateful for them!:

A birthday brings mixed feelings — some are happy,
      some are sad;
The young want to be older, others are and now feel
      bad.
But every birthday's special and whatever we may feel,
The surprise of a birthday card is pleasant, sweet and
      real.
So when you give a little thought and write your
      wishes there,
Someone feels glad, and if alone, knows that you love
      and care.
So let's thank God for birthdays, 'tho you'll stay at
      thirty-five,
For if we didn't have them, we'd never be alive!

THE writer Mark Twain once wrote a humorous account of keeping a diary. He told how the first pages were very full, but as the year went on, the entries grew more and more skimpy till one day he wrote only, "Got up, washed, went to bed." Further on it was simply, "Got up. Went to bed." He must have tired himself out!

Well, writing diaries may not be for all of us, but I can't understand people who say, "I wouldn't know what to write in a diary. Nothing much seems to happen."

What a confession that is, when as R. L. Stevenson said, "The world is so full of a number of things, I am sure we should all be as happy as kings."

SUNDAY—FEBRUARY 21.

SO let each one give as he purposes in his heart, not grudgingly or of necessity. 2 Corinthians 9:7

MONDAY—FEBRUARY 22.

NONE of us goes through life without disappointments, hardships, frustrations, sorrows, yet how differently people react to these circumstances. I was reminded of this by a "Thought for the Week" in a church leaflet which a friend sends me from time to time:

"The hard experiences of life are like stones — grindstones which wear away our patience and hope, or stepping stones on which we mount to fresh endeavour and new hope."

The choice is ours.

TUESDAY—FEBRUARY 23.

"LAUGHTER is the best medicine," they say and here is a story of laughter actually saving a life.

It is reputed that Dr Patrick Scougal, a 17th century Scottish bishop, was earnestly sought by an old woman to visit her sick cow. The prelate reluctantly consented, and, walking round the animal, said gravely, "If she lives, she lives, and if she dies, she dies, and I can do no more for her."

Not long afterwards, the bishop himself was dangerously afflicted with quinsy in the throat, whereupon the old woman, having gained access to his chamber, walked round his bed saying, "If he lives, he lives, and if he dies he dies, and I can do no more for him."

At this, the bishop was seized with a fit of laughter which burst the quinsy and saved his life!

INSPIRATION

On days when life's a slippery slope
The hills stand firm, renewing hope.

WEDNESDAY—FEBRUARY 24.

A POPULAR radio programme of many years ago was "The Brains Trust", in which experts in several fields were asked to give their answers on a variety of topics.

The philosopher, C. E. M. Joad, was noted for his wisdom. Once, he said:

"Happiness isn't to be found in the gospel of a good time. It consists rather in doing something which appears to you to be worthwhile, in being used up to the last ounce of your energy and capacity in the doing of it, and then looking back and noticing that you have been happy."

THURSDAY—FEBRUARY 25.

WHAT are the really valuable things in this life? Carol Wills knows and wrote to tell me:

The world has riches in large measure,
Diamonds, silver and gold,
But there is yet more splendid treasure
No chest nor vault can hold.

Eyes of crystal; wisdom's pearl;
A mind of jewelled thought;
A golden heart, a silver smile:
Such wealth can ne'er be bought.

FRIDAY—FEBRUARY 26.

THOMAS CARLYLE, the great 19th century Scottish writer, said: "Wonder is the basis of worship. Music can be part of that worship. It is a kind of articulate, unfathomable speech which leads one to the edge of the Infinite and compels one to gaze in."

THE FRIENDSHIP BOOK

FEW things are more exasperating than waiting a long time for a bus. The other day I stood in a queue with a friend for over half an hour. Seeing our bus in the distance at last, she exclaimed: "How wonderful!" And when she stepped onto it she gave the driver a bright smile, remarking, "I *am* pleased to see you!"

How could she be in such a good mood when the rest of us were quietly fuming?

"I used to get so angry waiting at bus stops," she explained, "until I realised my anger was quite unproductive. Now I try to channel all my energies into feeling grateful that the bus has arrived. It makes me feel a lot better!"

And judging by the driver's warm smile, her good temper made his work a lot more cheerful, too.

AND whatever you do, do it heartily, as to the Lord and not to men.   Colossians 3:23

AFTER James Ramsay MacDonald lost his wife, he often used to recall the long walks they had taken together round Lossiemouth, the little town in Moray where they lived. He told how Mrs MacDonald would sometimes say, "Don't let's speak. Let's be silent, for then we speak most truly."

Silence is often more expressive than words. At those times when we "just don't know what to say", silence and the grip of a hand can often say it all for us. Silence, as much as words, is the bond of true friendship.

MARCH

TUESDAY—MARCH 1.

*B*RA VE March is such a show-off month!
A gusty, blowing, hopeful month.
The north wind blows, the south wind blows,
And yet I think March really shows
That he intends to clear the ways
To make room for bright Summer days.

This is the month we hoe the weeds,
And sow with trust the tiny seeds.
March calls to each of us: "Prepare!
Rise up again, and show you care!"
Don't just Spring-clean the house, but find
Those cobwebs also in your mind.

Joyce Frances Carpenter.

WEDNESDAY—MARCH 2.

IT'S lovely to entertain friends — even if it means a big washing-up afterwards, which I can't say I look forward to!

The other night, we left the pans till last. I think a lot of people do. And if I had been on my own I might have filled the most difficult ones with soapy water and left them till morning.

The Lady of the House had other ideas.

"Francis," she said, "I remember a woman who had been a maid in a big house saying there are only two kinds of washers-up — the scrapers and the steepers. I'm one of the scrapers. Will you please pass me the scourer?"

I still believe there's a place for the steepers of the world, but I must admit we got those pots cleaned and put away in no time!

THE FRIENDSHIP BOOK

ALTHOUGH Dr Samuel Johnson achieved great fame as a writer, success did not come easily to him. His early days were a continual struggle against hardship and poverty.

Obviously, his great ability contributed to his eventual success, but I wonder whether it was not due also to his belief that, "It is worth a thousand pounds a year to have the habit of always looking on the best side of things."

We may not share Doctor Johnson's literary ability, but we *can* share his philosophy of life.

I LIKE the old legend which records how Jesus was once sitting with His disciples round a fire in the street. John, that beloved disciple, took a piece of charcoal and traced the outline of his Master's shadow where it was thrown on the wall of a house.

Next day, many people stopped to inspect the outline, and guess who it represented. One man pointed to the crooked back and thought it depicted a shoemaker; his neighbour thought it had the likeness of a fruit-vendor. Along came a learned Pharisee who thought it was like himself — with the fine brow of a thinker.

Then came a poor and humble man with a strong, tender face, kind eyes, and a beautiful smile. He examined the outline closely, then exclaimed: "Oh, if only I could look like that! But that would be impossible." And as he stood there, the crowd hushed, and drew back, pointing to him.

For, without knowing it, the stranger did resemble the picture. He had lived a good life, and so he had come to look like Jesus.

THE FRIENDSHIP BOOK

MRS WILLIAMS from down the road told me about a conversation she'd had last week with her little daughter, Sarah.

"Have you got a big box, please, Mummy?" Sarah asked.

"What for?" inquired her mother.

"I want to send Her Majesty the Queen some plums," she replied.

"That's a nice thought, dear," said Mrs Williams. "But why?"

"Because in school yesterday," said Sarah, "we sang, 'Send her Victorias'!"

USE hospitality one to another without grudging.

I Peter 4:9

PHILOSOPHERS often seem to speak a language that we ordinary folk find difficult to understand. Yet many of them are capable, too, of expressing great truths very simply.

Here, for example, is something Bertrand Russell once wrote: "The happy life must to a great extent be a quiet life for it is only in an atmosphere of quiet that true joy can live."

Of course, quietness and stillness are not always easily come by in this busy, noisy world in which we live. A friend of mine is fond of saying, "It's no good trying to *find* time for peace and quiet; we have to *make* time for it."

Well, that's my resolution for today; how about you?

THE FRIENDSHIP BOOK

ISOBEL BAILLIE'S beautiful voice made her known in homes all over the land. But with her fame went a remarkable humility.

The actress Beryl Reid tells in her autobiography how when she was a child she used to visit Isobel Baillie's home to play with her daughter.

Beryl's career took her away from Isobel Baillie until they happened to be on the same programme at the Albert Hall. The great singer told Beryl she followed her career and had seen everything she had done on the stage.

"But why didn't you come round to see me?" Beryl asked.

"Oh," said Isobel Baillie, "I didn't think you would remember me."

I FOUND these lines by Bob Miles in a church magazine:

Fast from criticism and feast on praise;
Fast from self-pity and feast on joy;
Fast from ill-temper and feast on peace;
Fast from resentment and feast on contentment;
Fast from jealousy and feast on love;
Fast from pride and feast on humility;
Fast from selfishness and feast on service;
Fast from fear and feast on faith.

The above was specially written for the season of Lent. But what a lot of wisdom there is in them and what a difference it would make to our own happiness and that of those around us if we applied it the whole year through.

THE FRIENDSHIP BOOK

I HAD been in to see a very good friend, Will Brown. Will had been much bothered with a rheumaticky shoulder so I was delighted to see him bend down and lift up a pile of books without any discomfort.

"It's the warm olive oil," he told me. "Nothing like it! I was stiff as a poker yesterday afternoon. Then last night Emma rubbed warm olive oil into my shoulder for half an hour. What a difference it made!"

When I left, Emma came down to the gate. "Your olive oil treatment has certainly done the trick," I said.

Emma smiled. "I'm afraid I'm a cheat, Francis. The bottle was just about empty — only a few drops left. I'd meant to get a refill. So I kept rubbing in those few drops. Will never noticed. He just said, 'Oh, that's lovely. What a difference!'

"You're not a cheat at all," I said. "You did the right thing."

You won't find these words on any bottle, but they're there in invisible letters in so many homes: "Apply with love".

Just as Emma did.

TODAY I would like to share with you a few thoughts sent to me by Mrs I. Bracken, of Ousby, Penrith:

Be careful what you wish for — your wishes may be granted.

The best helping hand is the one at the end of your arm.

Watch your tongue — it's in a wet place and likely to slip.

Money won't pay your fare to Heaven.

THE FRIENDSHIP BOOK

HERE is a poem for Mother's Day tomorrow from Georgina Hall of Oldham:

A Mother has the special gift of always speaking true,
A mother gets the praise or blame if skies be dark or blue;
Mother is a doctor, a joiner or a vet,
The jobs a mother cannot do have not been heard of yet.

A Mother is a power all wise, a tyrant or a saint,
An oracle, a paragon, with smart ideas or quaint;
Whatever else she may be, a mother knows full well,
A house could never be a home without her magic spell.

BEHOLD, children are a heritage from the Lord.
Psalms 127:3

EMIL METTLER, the owner of a restaurant in London, was not remembered amongst his friends and neighbours for what he said, but for what he did. He was well known and loved for his cheerful generosity.

One day, a friend stood near as Emil opened the cash register, and was astonished to see among the notes and coins a six-inch nail. He asked about it, thinking that it should not be there. Emil smiled. Oh, yes, he explained, he always kept it there. It reminded him of the price Christ paid for his Salvation — "and what I owe Him in return."

HAVE you seen the famous picture of Jesus with the children of the world close around him? Many years ago it hung on my bedroom wall, but it was only recently that I heard this story about it.

The picture was almost finished and the artist had gone to bed when he was disturbed by the feeling that somebody was in his studio. He imagined that a man was there, in front of his picture, with a paint brush in his hand. "Stop," cried the artist, "you will ruin my picture!"

"You have ruined it already," said the stranger, continuing to paint. "You have given all the children white faces and in heaven there are children with black faces, and brown ones and yellow ones, so I am putting it right for you."

Then the artist realised the stranger was Jesus, and as he did so, the figure vanished from sight.

In the morning, the artist hurried to his studio, but the picture was just as he had left it the night before. Picking up his brushes and paint he began to work quickly. Soon the picture was completed in the way it should have been, with a little Chinese child, a Negro, an Arab, an Indian and one little white girl — all gathered round the knee of their Saviour.

WEDNESDAY—MARCH 16.

I FOUND this verse in the pages of a church magazine which a friend sent to me. Its message speaks for itself:

> *"I could have made a better world,"*
> *A cynic to a saint once cried;*
> *"And that is why God put you here:*
> *Go forth and do it," he replied.*

THE FRIENDSHIP BOOK

MANY years ago there was a popular song with the title "I Want To Be Happy". Don't we all? Happiness, gladness, joy, pleasure, cheerfulness, delight — these are but a few of the terms to describe the state of mind most people would like to have.

If we look up those words in the dictionary we find there is a certain overlapping of meaning. On the other hand, I think there is also a subtle difference between many of them. For example, someone once pointed out the difference between happiness and cheerfulness. He said, "A happy person has no cares at all; a cheerful person has cares but has learned how to deal with them."

WE'VE just had Peter, a local painter and decorator, in the house and I couldn't help but remark on his family's renowned cheerfulness. He grinned and then handed me a copy of a "family contract" written by his grandparents, the founders of his business, many years ago. It read:

"At home we employ a *thick coat* of genuine *emotion;* there's no *whitewash* or *gloss*ing over — and no *veneer;* we don't need to *paper over the cracks* because we encourage all *shades* of honest feelings to be *exposed* and *harmonised.* Nobody gets *stirred* up, *stained, brushed* up the wrong way, or loses *distemper* since a *pure mixture* of absolute truth and sincerity *mellows* to *weatherproof* against any *roughcast* our way. An *unvarnished* family *spirit enriches* its members and *renders* a *bright, cheerful tone over-all.* Beware of *substitutes!*"

A good mix, I'd say, for *any* family wishing to appear in its true colours!

PRECIOUS MOMENTS

In savouring simple joys you will
Capture the rapture of time held still.

THE FRIENDSHIP BOOK

CATHERINE BRAMWELL-BOOTH, one of the grand-daughters of the founder of the Salvation Army, William Booth, was surely one of the most remarkable women of our time. She was still preaching when she was 100 years old and on that memorable birthday took part in several television interviews.

Asked about the secret of happy living she said, "If you haven't learned to love someone better than you love yourself you haven't even begun to live."

A simple secret perhaps, but how greatly it was exemplified in the life of that very wonderful person.

THEREFORE do not worry about tomorrow, for tomorrow will worry about its own things.

Matthew 6:34

IF you've ever made bread you'll know how important is the kneading of the dough. It's really a two-handed job.

A minister I know is renowned among his congregation for the brown bread he makes. No local good cause is complete without a loaf or two from his kitchen.

But there's something very special about his bread: he kneads the dough with one hand!

Why make things difficult for himself, you may wonder. Well, that's simple. He's a very busy man, and he likes to do his baking when he has the house to himself. So, just to be ready to deal with a phone call, he always keeps one hand out of the dough!

D

THE FRIENDSHIP BOOK

IN Fourteen hundred and ninety two,
Columbus sailed the ocean blue.

Perhaps you remember the old rhyme from your schooldays. But I wonder if you have heard this story which is attributed to Christopher Columbus?

When he returned to Spain after discovering America, he was feted wherever he went. One small group of nobles, however, was piqued at his success and tried to disparage him, saying that it was a simple thing to have done.

Columbus picked up an egg and asked each of them if he could stand it on end. In turn they all tried, without success.

Columbus took the egg himself and tapped the end gently until the shell was slightly flattened. Then he placed the egg on its end and it remained steady. "So you see, gentlemen," said Columbus, "anything is simple — if you know how to do it!"

BILLY BUTLIN brought happiness to millions of people through his famous holiday camps, but in a very much less public way he also brought happiness to thousands more through his generous benefactions to charitable causes.

Although much in the public eye, he was not very fond of speech-making. He used to say, jokingly, that he had only two speeches for public occasions — a short one and a long one. The short one was, "Thank you"; the long one was, "Thank you very much!"

We may not be much in the way of being public speakers ourselves, but I don't think we shall go far wrong if we can master those two speeches, and really mean it when we use them.

THE FRIENDSHIP BOOK

A MINISTER once told of the lady who had a little card pinned above her kitchen sink with the words "Divine Service held here three times daily".

The message there was that although we can't all be preachers, teachers or missionaries, we all have a job to do and we are able to honour God in the way we perform it.

I think this verse puts it very nicely:

> *Lord of all pots and pans and things,*
> *Since I've no time to be*
> *A saint by doing lovely things,*
> *Or watching late with Thee,*
> *Or dreaming in the dawn light,*
> *Or storming Heaven's gates,*
> *Make me a saint by getting meals*
> *And washing up the plates.*

J.H.B. PEEL has brought delight to thousands of readers through his books, "People and Places", "Country Talk", "More Country Talk" and many others.

He has walked the length and breadth of Britain and enjoys the quiet places, and deplores that so many of them have been spoiled by the noise and rush of tourist traffic — people, he says ruefully, "determined to see as little as possible as quickly as maybe!"

How aptly that phrase sums up the haste, bustle and restlessness of so many people even when they are supposed to be on holiday. It's a danger I think, in which many of us are apt to be caught up. Next time I am at leisure I am determined to see as *much* as possible as *slowly* as maybe. In fact, I'll try and snatch a few moments to do it today.

THE FRIENDSHIP BOOK

THE Lady of the House and I both like to sit down to a meal with a family which says grace.

The asking of a blessing on our food, reminds me, even if only for a few seconds, that I haven't an automatic right to three meals a day. Our forefathers, just two or three generations ago, dependent on the success of the local harvests, knew that very well.

When I was in a friend's house the other day, four-year-old Peter was asked to say grace and he piped up with one I hadn't heard before:

For every cup and every plateful,
Lord, we would be truly grateful.

It's really all that needs to be said, isn't it?

LET all things be done decently and in order.
I Corinthians 14:40

THE late Rev. W. Bardsley Brash, who was a Methodist minister and College Principal, often, in his writings, paid tribute to the saintliness and gaiety of spirit of his father, qualities which, Brash says, greatly influenced his own life. His father's religion, he said, had no place in it for gloom.

After the old man had been bedridden for some time, he died quite suddenly and peacefully with no-one present in his room. Lying beside him on his bedcover was his Bible — and a copy of "Punch"!

Holiness and happiness, goodness and gaiety — can there be any better combination for life?

EVER NEW

Isn't it amazing,
*   Though you've seen it all before,*
How beauty still surprises
*   When Spring holds wide the door.*

THE FRIENDSHIP BOOK

DO you believe all those stories about couples who, when celebrating silver or ruby wedding anniversaries, say "We've never had a cross word in all our years together?"

I was amused to read of one lady who, speaking of 50 years of marriage, said in answer to a question about this, "Well, we always have one at the breakfast table — the crossword we do together in the newspaper!"

THE Chinese have an ancient legend about a statesman, Liu Kuan, who was one day commanded to appear before the Emperor. It was to be an important meeting and he put on his court dress of intricately embroidered satin. Shortly before he set off, he ordered a new slave girl to bring him a bowl of hot soup.

The girl did so, but as she approached she tripped and the soup went over his robe. She burst into tears and cowered, expecting a blow. Instead Liu Kuan asked gently, "Have you scalded your hand?"

THE gardening writer Julian Meade once said, "If you want to know whether you are a welcome visitor to other people's gardens, test your character thus: Can you stand by your neighbour's border five minutes without saying 'I — me — my — mine'?

I like the idea of that simple test. I think it would be worth while trying it out on a few other things besides gardens. It could teach us all a bit more appreciation of "you" and "yours".

APRIL

FRIDAY—APRIL 1.

EASTER, in the Spring of the year when the earth is being renewed in beauty, speaks to us of the victory of life over death, and the defeat of darkness.

In Liverpool Anglican Cathedral is a memorial tablet which says simply, but triumphantly: "Here lies in honour all that could die of a pioneer of orthopaedic surgery, Sir Robert Jones."

What reassuring words these are — "all that could die"! They remind us of our faith in rebirth and the resurrection we celebrate this weekend.

A happy Easter to you all!

SATURDAY—APRIL 2.

HERE is a poem for Spring by Silvie Taylor of Dundee:

This morning I drew back the curtains—
Grey skies and a downpour of rain,
But, a glimmer of gold in the border:
The crocus are with us again!

Beside them, the last of the snowdrops,
Delicate heralds of Spring;
And high overhead in the cherry
A blackbird had started to sing.

For days now the sun has been hiding,
But we don't really need skies of blue.
The world is remarkably cheerful—
Well, that's how I see it. Do you?

ARISE, shine; for thy light is come, and the glory of the Lord is risen upon thee.   Isaiah 60:1

MONDAY—APRIL 4.

BRIAN JOHNSTON, who over the years delighted millions of listeners with his radio programme "Down Your Way" is, of course, also a well-known cricket commentator, and an enthusiast for the game.

"I am a great optimist," he once said. "Every time I go to a cricket match I think it is going to be the best game I have ever seen. Of course, it never is — but what pleasure it gives me in anticipation!"

A meal, a book, an outing, a concert, a holiday — what a lot of difference it can make if we think these are going to be the best we have ever had!

TUESDAY—APRIL 5.

MOST of us must at some time have said to ourselves, "I could have bitten my tongue when I said that." But it is too late, of course, and no matter what we do or say, the ill-considered, hurtful words cannot be unsaid.

The Quakers, those masters of silent prayer, have a useful little trio of questions which we might well get into the habit of thinking about before uttering any doubtful words:

1. Is this true?
2. Is it kind?
3. Is it necessary?

Three questions which could save others — and ourselves — a lot of pain.

THE FRIENDSHIP BOOK

I DON'T know if you have ever read Arnold Bennett's very funny novel, "The Card". The hero of the story, Denry Machin, is born the son of a washerwoman and rises to be the Mayor of the town, achieving this by various impudent devices and manoeuvres.

Not everybody in the story loves Denry. Some, jealous of his success, positively detest him, but he is generally a popular figure.

The reason for his popularity is summed up at the end of the book. "He's identified," said an admirer, "with the great cause of cheering us all up."

We can't all be Mayor, and perhaps we wouldn't want to be, but we can still emulate Denry Machin. There's always room in our lives for more cheerfulness.

AS I walked down the road, the swans which nest on the island in the middle of the pond nearby, were making their way across the road to the house where they are fed every day. It won't be long before they will be taking their seven or eight new cygnets along also.

There are a number of houses near the pond, but the swans return to this particular one year after year because they are never refused food.

People, too, need a haven, somewhere they can go, knowing there is someone there who will have time for a chat, or even provide a shoulder to cry on. There is always room in any neighbourhood for a home with the welcome sign up. It could be mine, it could be yours — and the results of such friendships can often be surprisingly rewarding.

THE FRIENDSHIP BOOK

YOUNG Billy loves to try out his latest puzzle on me. I think he knows I am not very good at them and nearly always have to give in.

"Mr Gay," he asked, "which dog has most tails, one dog or no dog?"

"That's easy," I said. "If there's no dog there's no tail."

"But that's where you're wrong, Mr Gay. One dog has one tail. No dog has two tails. So no dog has one tail more than one dog!"

IN April 1764, Leopold Mozart brought his musically talented son, Wolfgang, to London, at that time the musical capital of Europe. Wolfgang was only seven years old, but he was soon giving public concerts on the organ and harpsichord.

During the Summer of that year, they settled in Chelsea where Leopold became very ill. As he needed peace and quiet, Wolfgang was not allowed to play his instruments and friends took him instead to visit the famous Chelsea Bun House, the Tower and Westminster Abbey. Between times, the little boy composed his very first symphony (K 16). This, and his other London compositions, are now gathered together in an album called the "Chelsea Notebook".

It is said that, after each public performance, Wolfgang would go to the front of the platform and, as he modestly took his bow, would give the audience a big smile.

"Then I get lots and lots of smiles back," he told his father.

The little boy had worked hard and found the true measure of happiness at an early age.

THE FRIENDSHIP BOOK

AND the peace of God, which passeth all understanding, shall keep your hearts and minds through Jesus Christ.

Philippians 4:7

QUEEN VICTORIA is remembered as one who was not amused, but there was one occasion when she most certainly was. It was at Crathie Church, near Balmoral Castle, and the minister, the Rev. James MacGregor, appealed in his prayer to the Almighty to "send down his wisdom on the Queen's ministers — who sorely need it".

I don't know if she agreed with him or not, but it is recorded that she shook with suppressed laughter!

ONE morning a man took his son with him on a shooting expedition. The father, shooting at a partridge and not seeing his son, hit him in the face, causing instant blindness.

The young man faced up to life with its new limitations, and eventually entered Parliament.

The time came when Gladstone made him Postmaster General, and said of him, "His heroic acceptance of blindness has left a memorable example of the power of a brave man to turn loss into gain, and wrest victory from misfortune."

The man in question, Henry Fawcett, said simply, "Blindness is an inconvenience, not a tragedy."

It would have been easy for him to surrender to despair, self-pity, or bitterness. Instead, he "turned loss into gain . . . and wrested victory from misfortune."

SEA PINKS

THE FRIENDSHIP BOOK

IN some parts of England, Mop Fairs are still held annually. Nowadays these are simply for pleasure, but originally they were for the hiring of labour of various kinds. Those offering their services would wear a symbol appropriate to their work — housemaids carrying mops, milkmaids with dairy pails, carters with whips, shepherds with crooks or a wisp of wool in their hats, and so on.

Agreements were entered into, but sometimes masters or servants might have second thoughts and wish to terminate the contract as soon as possible. So, in many places, a week or a fortnight later, there was a Runaway Mop Fair at which either party could withdraw.

It's just a quaint old custom — yet it is a reminder of how grateful we ought to be that life continually offers us second chances, fresh starts, forgiveness, renewal.

TO an earlier generation, the film star Mary Pickford was known as the "World's Little Sweetheart".

In later years, as a statement of her Christian faith, she wrote a book, "Why Not Try God?" Here is a thought from it:

"Today is a new day. You will get out of it just what you put into it. If you have made mistakes, even serious mistakes, there is always another chance for you.

"And supposing you have tried and failed again and again, you may have a fresh start any moment you choose, for this thing we call failure is not the falling down, but the staying down."

FRIDAY—APRIL 15.

I WAS impressed with this thoughtful and practical prayer written by Clemency Greatorix:
Teach us to listen Lord . . .
To one another with enjoyment and especially:
To the diffident with encouragement,
To the sad with understanding,
To the repetitive with patience,
To the happy, joyfully,
To the aggressive, calmly;
But to the gossip — never.

It occurred to me that the first six requests are the ones that are easiest for us to carry out, whilst it is often the hardest thing in the world not to enjoy a bit of gossip.

Can we make it our resolution to try to put *all* of it into practice?

SATURDAY—APRIL 16.

LEN HUTTON'S name is known wherever cricket is played. His record innings of 364 for England in a test match has stood for over 45 years.

But Len, later Sir Leonard, of course — always had his feet firmly on the ground. In a match some time after he had made his famous score, he was clean bowled for a duck. As he left the field to a shocked silence from the crowd, somebody called to him from the pavilion steps, "What happened, Len?"

"What happened?" said Len. "Well, I missed it, didn't I?"

SUNDAY—APRIL 17.

FOR we walk by faith, not sight.

II Corinthians 5:7

THE FRIENDSHIP BOOK

ASK any native or regular visitor to the Lake District to recommend a book of poetry or essays on this beautiful area, and they are likely to suggest one by Norman Nicholson.

It is something of a miracle that he was able to write any books at all. Young Norman was so often ill that in his "Portrait of the Lakes" he confesses, "Too much of my youth had to be spent trying to save my life for me to see much fun in risking it on rocks or in water."

That was merely his way of stating his long struggle with ill-health. However, he survived to write numerous books and volumes of poetry, all adding to the richness of Lakeland tapestry.

Many of his remembrances are of the tiny port and iron town of Millom, where his father owned an outfitting business. His expert knowledge of customs and the love of his native area, so wonderfully expressed in his books, has made it known as "Norman Nicholson Country".

He did not need to travel so very far from home to discover riches to write about. They were found in his own countryside, its Nature and people.

A BRIEF, easy-to-remember prayer from an anonymous author in mediaeval times may help you, as it has often helped me:

> *Where love is,*
> *There riches be.*
> *Keep us all*
> *From poverty.*

How rich we are if we love and are loved.

THE FRIENDSHIP BOOK

THE church at Lower Quinton in Warwickshire has beautiful stained glass windows which at first sight may seem little different from many others. Look at them closely, however, and you'll see that they depict butterflies, insects, elves in snail shells and many birds, including a wren, an owl and a swallow.

The windows were commissioned by the Rev. Gordon Poole, who was vicar there from 1911 to 1932. When they were being designed, he and the artist, Geoffrey Webb, asked the village children what they would like included in the design.

It was a lovely idea, for as the children grew up they could look at their own childhood fancies in those windows. We can't all have our memories captured in stained glass, but it is good sometimes to go back in imagination, "across the years long-vanished" and reflect on our thoughts and dreams of yesterday.

IN the Middle Ages, people crossed the English Channel frequently. Not only did they take part in the Crusades, but many travelled with their lords and masters, visiting lands they owned on both sides of the water. In fact, people in those days looked on the Channel exactly as its name implies, as a means of channelling them to and fro, from one part of their land to another. It was only much later in history that people began to think of the Channel as separating Britain from the rest of Europe.

Relationships can be like that, too. We can either go through life each following our separate ways, or we can let ourselves become channels for the to and fro of friendship and love. As St Francis wrote in his prayer, "Make me a channel of your peace."

D

THRILLING

When the wonder of childhood springs to life
And a magical castle appears,
What dreams there are,
What schemes there are
And every lad with a wanderlust
The call of adventure hears.

FRIDAY—APRIL 22.

OUR friend, Henry, who is 70 next birthday, tends to be a bit gloomy about the prospects of growing old. A group of us was talking together the other day and he told us that he and his wife were planning a holiday in France. He sighed, "I reckon, at my age, it will be our last trip abroad."

One of our company, much older in years than Henry, but younger in spirit, said, "Now, Henry, that's no way to talk. You ought to be planning to do things for the *first* time, not talking about doing them for the *last!*"

He had the right idea!

SATURDAY—APRIL 23.

WHEN we think of St. George, whose festival day this is, we almost certainly think of him in connection with the dragon he is supposed to have slain.

But there is a less well-known yet more factual incident connected with Saint George. The Emperor Constantine built a church over the saint's grave and declared him the guardian of seaside towns, ships, channels and dangerous waters, hence the St. George's Channel between England and Wales.

We owe so much to those who protect our shores, fish in the deep seas, and bring supplies across perilous waters, that we might well give this St. George's Day a rather fresh angle by giving special thought and prayer "For those in peril on the sea."

SUNDAY—APRIL 24.

WE then that are strong ought to bear the infirmities of the weak, and not to please ourselves.   Romans 15:1

THE FRIENDSHIP BOOK

WE all find ourselves waiting at some time or other —for buses and trains, waiting for someone who is late for an appointment, waiting in queues. It can be irritating, but a friend has made up a little rhyme which he says reminds him how to take the frustration out of waiting.

He refuses to fuss and fret. Instead he fixes his mind on some pleasant thing and meditates on that.

And the little verse which reminds him what to do?

I don't just wait;
I meditate!

I've tried it and it works!

THE late John Masefield, who became Poet Laureate, used to tell of a mystical experience he had when he was 31. He was feeling frustrated because his work had not achieved the success he felt it should have done, and one Spring morning he went for a lonely walk and saw the first primrose of the season.

His spirits immediately rose and he heard a voice saying, "Spring is beginning." He felt it meant not only the season of the year but the beginning of a new phase in his life. Shortly afterwards he wrote "The Everlasting Mercy" which helped to establish him as a poet.

Ever afterwards, April had a special meaning for him. The word appears dozens of times in his poems — "April's a wondrous thing", "April, a dear delight", "April's in the west wind and daffodil", "Somewhere in every heart it's April still".

May this April day bring uplift of spirits and new beginnings for us all.

SPLENDID PAGEANTRY

THE FRIENDSHIP BOOK

YEARS ago I copied down in one of my notebooks the words of an anonymous writer who said that true happiness is less the result of what we call the outstanding events of our lives, which are rare, than of the everyday experiences, which are common.

He wrote, "Everyday feelings which decide the colour of our lives — family ties, friends, books, flowers, food, water, the wind, health, shelter, sleep, the open road, rain in summer, fire in winter, dawn, songs, the starry sky, love in youth and memory in old age: are not these vast commonplaces the very gist of life?"

THE rich industrialist from the North was horrified to find the Southern fisherman lying lazily beside his boat, smoking a pipe.

"Why aren't you out fishing?" asked the rich man.

"Because I have caught enough fish for the day," replied the fisherman.

"Why don't you catch more than you need?" asked the industrialist.

"What would I do with it?" said the fisherman.

"You could earn more money," was the reply. "You could use it to have a motor fixed to your boat. Then you could go into deeper waters and catch more fish. Then you would make enough to buy nylon nets. These would bring you more fish and more money. Soon you would have enough money to own two boats. Then you would be a rich man like me."

"What would I do then?" asked the fisherman.

"Then you could sit down and enjoy life," said the industrialist.

"What do you think I'm doing right now?" asked the contented fisherman.

FRIDAY—APRIL 29.

I LIKE this thought sent to me from a reader in Canada:

Wouldn't our days be drear and long
If all went right and nothing wrong;
And wouldn't our world be dull and flat,
If there was nothing to grumble at?

SATURDAY—APRIL 30.

"YOU want a job, do you?" asked the American.

The former cabin boy, who had travelled from Liverpool to New Orleans, nodded.

The questioner smiled. "Tell me something about yourself," he suggested.

The lad told him that he had been born in 1841 in Denbigh, Wales. His mother had left him in a workhouse, and as he grew older he set out to find her. He did so, but she had married and did not want him in her life.

After this he became a cabin boy and landed in America. Now he was applying for an errand boy's job with a Mississippi trader called Stanley.

He got the job, and so hard did he work and so eager was he too please his new friend and employer, that Stanley decided to adopt him, giving him the name Henry Morton Stanley.

That was the beginning of the adventurous life of the man whose successful expedition found the lost Dr David Livingstone in Africa. His words "Dr Livingstone, I presume?" are famous. Stanley himself became celebrated as a writer and explorer.

He had few early advantages, but he made the most of any opportunities that came along, and left his mark on the pages of history.

MAY

ASK, and it shall be given you; seek, and ye shall find.

Matthew 7:7

TAKE enthusiasm and patience, coupled with hard work and study, and it is amazing what people can achieve.

There was Roy Grant, for example. Many years ago, he began to take a keen interest in mediaeval history, art and literature. Not content with studying these, he was fired with ambition to own a mediaeval hall and furnish it in keeping with its age. The 13th century St. Oswald's Old Church in York is Roy's dream come true.

For years he searched all over England before he discovered St. Oswald's. After much negotiation, dozens of plans, and applications to various planning authorities, a firm of local builders set to work on the transformation under the expert guidance of a London architect.

Now, the exterior, set in the old churchyard, looks unaltered. Inside, though, it is like stepping back centuries. Around you are authentic wall hangings, pictures and furniture. Only the kitchen and bathroom under the tower, and the study-library in the gallery overlooking the former nave are modern.

Roy Grant describes himself as its guardian and allows people to visit his mediaeval hall on certain dates in the year.

Perseverance will achieve just about anything, as Roy's success proves.

QUIET WATERS

Welcome blessing from God the Giver:
Cool, calm pools of a Highland river.

THE FRIENDSHIP BOOK

SOME go to church just for a walk;
Some go to laugh, some to talk;
Some go there for speculation;
Some go there for observation;
Some go there to meet a friend;
Some the tedious hours to spend;
Some to learn the parson's name;
Some go there to wound his fame;
Some go there to meet a lover;
Some, new fashions to discover;
Some go there to doze or nod;
But few go there to worship God!

Cynical, did you say? Yes — but it was found in an old Prayer Book of 1870!

ENJOYING the beauty of flowers sometimes brings to mind the old legends connected with them.

One story, not so well-known, is about the pretty little blue forget-me-not. It is said that Adam was walking in the Garden of Eden giving names to various plants and flowers. He overlooked the little plant although it was stretching up as far as possible to be noticed. Suddenly "the first gardener" heard God's voice asking him what name he was giving to the little flower.

Adam could not think of a suitable one, so the Creator suggested that of "forget-me-not" to remind him that, even though tiny, the small plant, like all small things, should not be ignored.

Only a legend? Yes, but it is a pleasant tale to remember when admiring forget-me-nots.

THE FRIENDSHIP BOOK

SOMEONE once said, "Great men forget themselves. That is why they are remembered by others." Most of us are unlikely to have our names in the history books or even in the headlines of the newspapers, but there is a kind of "greatness" we can all share — greatness of heart, being remembered by others because we have forgotten ourselves.

We can be numbered among the people whom a poet called, "the heroes the world has never known."

AS we flick through brochures from the travel agencies, dreaming of holidays in faraway places, I wonder how many of us spare a thought for the man who started it all — Thomas Cook?

He had the insight to discover a new need and the opportunity to provide for it, and it came about because of his lifelong zeal for temperance.

In 1841, as he walked 15 miles to a meeting, he was thinking of the news that the Midland Railway had opened a new local line. Later he wrote, "I reflected on what a glorious thing it would be if the newly-developed powers of railways could be made subservient to the promotion of temperance."

The idea was born, and he hired trains to take delegates to meetings. As Cook's plans developed, he organised day excursions, Scottish holidays, and the thing that had always been his ideal, cheap holidays for lower paid workers. By 1864 he was arranging European travel, and by 1872 what he called his "crowning achievement" — a world tour.

At his birthplace in Melbourne, Derbyshire, he is remembered in a simple tablet that reads "He made world travel easier".

THE FRIENDSHIP BOOK

IT was an anonymous poet who told us how he — or she — always looked on the bright side:

> *The inner side of every cloud*
> *Is bright and shining;*
> *I therefore turn my clouds about*
> *And always wear them inside out —*
> *To show the lining.*

Charles Kingsley gave us this advice on how to see the best this world has to offer us:

"Never lose an opportunity," he said, "to see anything beautiful. Beauty is God's handwriting."

LORD, hear my voice! Let Your ears be attentive to the voice of my supplications. — Psalms 30:2

THROUGHOUT the centuries, man has sought the elixir of youth. Much advice has been given, including these hints from an "expert" in Seattle, USA. Under the heading, "Three Golden Rules for Staying Young", we read the following:

Mix with other people.

Keep up intellectual exercises like reading and doing crossword puzzles.

Seek new experiences, if only simple ones like occasionally visiting a new restaurant.

These are sensible enough, but surely the advice of Charles Dickens shows a warmer and more human approach: "Have a heart that never hardens, and a temper that never tires, and a touch that never hurts."

HIGHLAND TRANQUILLITY

THE FRIENDSHIP BOOK

THERE is a beautiful story about a gift fit for a king. Many years ago, the King of Persia used to go on journeys to various parts of his realm, to see how his people were faring. On these journeys, his subjects were expected to give him a handsome present as an indication of their loyalty.

One day, he was approaching a farmer working in his fields. The man was dismayed. He was a long way from his house and did not know what to give the king. Then he had an idea. He rushed to the stream which ran through his meadow, gathered up some water in his cupped hands and held it out to the king saying, "Your Majesty, I would like to give you a really fine gift as a token of my love and loyalty, but at the moment I have nothing to offer except this drink of water. I give it with all my heart."

The farmer feared the king would be angry. Instead he drank the water gratefully and said, "I am pleased to accept your gift. It is your best and no man can give me any finer gift than that."

A FAMILY moved into a new district and a lady who lived across the road welcomed them by bringing a bunch of flowers picked from her garden. The recipient was so delighted, she made up her mind that, whenever anybody else moved into the street, she would do the same for them.

A lady who lived near an orphanage decided that, every time she baked cakes or scones she would do a few extra and hand them in. Others in the neighbourhood heard about this and they began to do it, too.

Good ideas are like weeds — they spread quickly!

THE FRIENDSHIP BOOK

TITUS AURELIUS FLUVIUS BOIONIUS ARRIUS was a Roman Emperor of the second century AD. You might think that such a collection of names could have been a disadvantage but, in fact, he was greatly loved by his people, for his nature bestowed upon them an era of outstanding peace and prosperity.

When he was on his deathbed, Marcus Aurelius, who was to be his successor, came with a group of Roman dignitaries. Anxiously they asked the Emperor to explain to them his code of living — the philosophy responsible for all the tranquillity and other benefits of his reign. He was silent for quite a long time and then uttered one word, "Equanimity."

What better word to fit our needs today?

FOR many years Mother Teresa and the sisters of her community have devoted themelves to helping the poor and needy in Calcutta. Once, speaking about her work, she said, "It's only a drop in the ocean — but the ocean wouldn't be the same without that drop."

There is a Mexican prayer which expresses a similar thought:

I am only a spark — make me a fire.
I am only a string — make me a lyre.
I am only a drop — make me a fountain.
I am only an anthill — make me a mountain.
I am only a feather — make me a wing.
I am only a rag — make me a king!

How our smallest efforts are magnified when the motives behind them are unselfish!

THE FRIENDSHIP BOOK

I THINK that of all the many tributes paid to Robert Louis Stevenson for the way he triumphed over pain and sickness, the most moving is that of another writer, G. K. Chesterton, who said, "He never let the smell of his medicine bottle get into his writing".

It would have been easy for him to allow self-pity to creep into his work. He never did. When we are so tempted, we would do well to remember Robert Louis Stevenson's medicine bottle — and how he left it firmly in the medicine cabinet.

BE ready, for the Son of Man is coming at an hour when you do not expect Him.   Matthew 24:44

RECENTLY my friend Edwin wrote telling me of a visit he made to a certain New York department store where one of the sales staff, Mary Peterson, is a girl who obviously loves her job. Her voice and the expression on her face show how she enjoys her work.

To her, the most important thing is helping people. As a result, customers don't mind waiting for up to half an hour just for the pleasure of being served by her. My friend tells me that he has never enjoyed buying something for his wife as much as the new sweater he bought from Mary.

What has made Mary such an outstanding member of the sales staff? Her lifelong basic philosophy is that the surest way to make your work enjoyable is to dedicate yourself to serving others with all your heart and soul.

E

THE FRIENDSHIP BOOK

A YOUNG man was being interviewed for a job as a street sweeper. He asked whether he would be given any special training.

"Nothing special," came the reply. "You'll have to pick it up as you go along!"

THE poet Barbara Jemison wrote to me recently: "There are many verses written about little girls, but not so many about boys." She enclosed this poem in which she expresses her feelings about them. I'm delighted to share it with you:

> *Short or tall, hefty or small,*
> *Little rogues, I love them all.*
> *Freckled face and ginger hair,*
> *Straight or curly, dark or fair,*
> *Grin of mischief, angel smile,*
> *Temper wild, charm to beguile.*
> *Pockets full of stones and string,*
> *Apple cores and many a thing*
> *Dear unto the hearts of boys:*
> *Knights and cowboys, trains and toys,*
> *Catching newts and climbing trees,*
> *Conkers, marbles, grubby knees,*
> *Sport and study, noise and fun,*
> *Examinations, matches won.*
> *Youth clubs, barbecues and such,*
> *Pop songs with romantic touch,*
> *Records, crew cuts, jeans and girls,*
> *Thus it is their life unfurls.*
> *Maddening at times, it's true,*
> *But so often thoughtful, too;*
> *Untidy, full of rush and noise,*
> *But what would life be without boys?*

F

THE FRIENDSHIP BOOK

A FRIEND of ours collects unusual "dedications" written by authors at the front of their books. One of his favourites is that by Bernie Smith in his book, "The Joy of Trivia". It reads:

"For Ruby, who for the past 27 years has been relentlessly belabouring me to do two things: (1) write this book and (2) fix the hinge on the driveway gates. Okay. Now to tackle that hinge . . . just as soon as I get a spare moment!"

HAVE you heard this story told by the writer, R. T. Moore?

A carpenter's tools were having a discussion and found themselves in conflict. Brother Hammer was trying to get order, but the others said he was far too noisy and would have to leave. "All right," he said, "but Brother Plane must withdraw, too, because there is no depth to his work."

Brother Plane responded, "Well, Brother Rule will also have to go. He's always measuring people as if he's the only one who's right."

Then Brother Rule complained about Brother Sandpaper because he was always rubbing people up the wrong way.

In the heat of the discussion, the Carpenter of Nazareth walked in, went to his bench and quietly began work on a pulpit from which he would preach the Gospel. He used the Hammer, the Plane, the Rule and the Sandpaper.

When the fine pulpit was completed, Brother Hammer spoke up again. "I see now that each one of us is a labourer for God," he said. "We each have our own part to play, but we must all play in harmony."

THE FRIENDSHIP BOOK

GRAN FARRELL was famous for her smile. All the children in the street warmed to it and so did her grandson Peter. The two-year-old couldn't help it, for whenever Gran caught a glimpse of him she would grin broadly, displaying her beautiful white teeth.

Once, Gran went to stay with Peter and his parents, and just before settling down for the night she took out her dentures and popped them into a glass of water. What a shock Peter had when he crept into her room for an early morning cuddle!

"Quick," he called to his parents, "Gran's smile is drowning!"

FOR who in the heavens can be compared to the Lord?
                                        Psalms 89:6

A FRIEND of Robert Baden-Powell, the founder of the Scout Movement, stayed with the great man when he was in his eighties. Getting up one morning at what he thought was a very early hour, he was surprised to find Baden-Powell already at work in his study.

Seeing the surprise on his guest's face, Baden-Powell said, "Oh, I get up at five every morning. By taking an extra hour each day I collect 365 hours per annum, or several weeks' advantage. I reckon that I get 54 weeks of life each year instead of 52."

Well, few of us, I imagine, would have the energy to emulate that, but what a lot we might gain by just an extra 10 minutes a day, for reading, or writing letters, or many another profitable use.

THE FRIENDSHIP BOOK

I WAS very impressed with these Beatitudes for Parents sent to me from Trinidad:

Blessed are the parents who can laugh at themselves, for their children will laugh with them and not at them.

Blessed are those who can see the world with the freshness and excitement of a small child, for they will always be young at heart.

Blessed are the parents of babies who can wake up joyful and clear of eye at 5.45 a.m., for they will have to get up at that hour anyway.

Blessed are they who spend adequate time caring for their children during infancy and childhood, for they shall be spared many teenage problems.

Blessed are the parents who take their children with them often, for they shall see the world with fresh eyes.

No doubt the above was written with a twinkle in the eye, but what a wealth of good sense there is here for parents — and for those of us who are grandparents, too!

AT the beginning of his career, Bernard Leach, the Cornish potter, spent about ten years working and studying his craft in Japan.

The thing that impressed him most was the Japanese insistence on "beauty for beauty's sake"; they created, not for utility, not for money, but simply for beauty.

I wonder if today each of us were to try to make something beautiful, or look at something beautiful, or even just think about something beautiful—the world might be a lovelier place by nightfall.

THURSDAY—MAY 26.

OUR friend Elsie Bruce has a son in Australia who was recently married there, but Elsie had not been able to attend the ceremony.

"Do you plan to visit your son and daughter-in-law?" the Lady of the House asked her the other day.

"Well, not just yet," replied Elsie. "I shall wait till, hopefully, they have their first child. You see, I have a theory that grandmas are more welcome than mothers-in-law!"

FRIDAY—MAY 27.

BARTHOLOMEW DIAZ was one of Portugal's greatest explorers. It was he who rounded the southernmost tip of Africa in 1488, in weather so rough that he named it Cabo Tormentoso — the Cape of Storms.

His King didn't think that he had given it the most encouraging sort of name. After all, how much traffic would a name like that attract?

So King John II of Portugal re-christened Africa's southernmost point by the optimistic name it bears today — The Cape of Good Hope.

SATURDAY—MAY 28.

THE minister stood up in church to give out the notices.

"I publish the banns of marriage between — " he began, then looked for his book with the necessary information but couldn't find it. "I publish the banns of marriage between — " he repeated, looking anxiously all around for the book.

The clerk leaned towards him and whispered loudly, "Between the cushion and the desk, sir!"

THE FRIENDSHIP BOOK

I SAY to you, inasmuch as you did it to one of the least of these My brethren, you did it to Me.

Matthew 25:40

WHEN Robinson Crusoe found a footprint in the sand, he felt sure that his lonely sojourn was about to be brought to an end.

It didn't matter to him who had made that footprint as long as its owner was friendly. It was just the fact that someone else was there on his island with him.

Often we see people on their own little islands of loneliness, yet we fail to take the small step necessary to make them feel less isolated in a hostile world. A smile, a wave or a kind word can so easily fill an empty moment in a lonely life.

We can make an impression in this way on any day of the week — we don't have to wait for a Friday!

I WONDER if you look forward, as I do, to the sound of mail dropping through the letter box? Of course sometimes the postman can bring bills and other unwelcome items, but I think it is the thought of the *unexpected* in my mail which gives me so much pleasure.

Many things have to be planned — meal-times, trains or buses to catch, appointments to keep and so on, but you never know what is in the post!

How dull life would be if it was *all* planned, if there were no surprises. I wonder what's in the post this morning . . .

JUNE

WEDNESDAY—JUNE 1.

SHEILA was immensely proud of her front garden and she'd every right to be. A busy wife and mother, she somehow found time to grow plants from seed so that in the summer a rainbow of colours brightened her end of the street.

"It gladdens my old heart," Alice from next door used to say. "The sight of those flowers really cheers me up."

Last year, Sheila's garden was even more colourful than usual, so you can imagine her horror when she looked out one stormy day and saw the borders bare of blooms. "I didn't think it had been all that windy," she thought, and then she wondered, how would old Alice take it?

She went round to see her neighbour and explain, and there she was, struggling with a huge armful of flowers — Sheila's flowers — and at her side was Sheila's youngest, a little girl of three, who was looking decidedly pleased with herself.

"I'm cheering her up," she beamed at her mother.

"I *was* proud of my garden," Sheila told her husband over supper, "but somehow I'm even prouder of our daughter."

THURSDAY—JUNE 2.

AFTER several years of less-than-average rainfall, and an increasing demand for water, plans were made to construct a new reservoir in Yorkshire. During a debate on the proposals, an objector remarked: "I don't see why you want a new reservoir — you can't fill the ones you've got now!"

THE FRIENDSHIP BOOK

I LOVE sundials, and what I especially like about them is that motto they often bear: "I count only the sunny hours".

Can we learn to be selective like that? How wonderful it would be if we could train ourselves when thinking about the past to let in only the thoughts of the happy times we have had. And how much better it would be for us and for those around us if we could shut out from our minds the memory of times when we have thought other people were being hurtful to us, and recall only the kindly words and deeds that have been said and done.

AN ancient fable tells of a king who was sad because his people were always complaining about their troubles. At last, he ordered them to assemble in the square in front of his palace.

"Take off your burdens," commanded the king, "and place them upon the ground in front of you. When you have done this, walk around and select for yourselves the troubles of others which seem least wearisome to you. However, you must leave no burden here for I have problems enough of my own."

The people did as they were told, but next day they all returned to the square in great distress. "Oh, King!" they cried. "Please give us back our old troubles because the new ones we have chosen are awkward and painful to carry."

The king graciously granted their request, telling them, "We all have burdens to carry in life, but the ones that come naturally to us are those which can be carried most comfortably because they are tailored exactly to fit our own backs."

THE FRIENDSHIP BOOK

SUNDAY—JUNE 5.

BLESSED are the peacemakers : for they shall be called the children of God.   Matthew 5:9

MONDAY—JUNE 6.

DR LESLIE WEATHERHEAD, the famous preacher, once arrived rather earlier than expected in a town with which he wasn't familiar. He had an evening engagement, and the only place he could find to pass the time was a public house opposite the church. He went in, ordered a glass of lemonade, and was soon in animated conversation with some of the customers.

As he rose to leave, one of the men said to him: "Sir, if the likes of you came in here more often, perhaps the likes of us would go in there oftener, too" — pointing to the church across the road.

TUESDAY—JUNE 7.

NIPPER was a little dog belonging to a London artist and photographer named Francis Barraud. When he was at work, Barraud liked to listen to music which he played on an early gramophone. Nipper seemed to like the music, too, for he would sit with his head cocked, gazing at the machine. Barraud painted a picture of him doing just that and submitted it to the Royal Academy. They did not accept it so he offered it to the Edison Bell Phonographic Company, whose machine was in the picture. They didn't want it either, but the rival Gramophone Company snapped it up at once, and used it in their advertising. The painting became famous under the title "His Master's Voice".

If Barraud is still remembered today, it's because of Nipper, the little dog that liked to listen to music.

THE FRIENDSHIP BOOK

THE German singer, Ernestine Schumann-Heink, had just started to sing at a concert when a baby lying in its mother's arms in the front row started to cry loudly. Greatly embarrassed, the mother rose to carry the child out, but Madame Schumann-Heink stopped singing, stepped to the front of the platform and said, "Sit down again, my dear. I have had seven children of my own and I can sing louder than any child can cry. Perhaps I'll sing a lullaby" — which she proceeded to do.

Not only was the large audience enraptured by this sympathetic act and the worried mother comforted — but the baby fell fast asleep!

A LITTLE while ago, when the Lady of the House and I were on a country walk, we stopped by the side of a stream to eat our sandwiches. As we sat there, we watched with amusement a group of children who were jumping backwards and forwards across the stream. It was neither very wide nor very deep, but just enough to make an exciting challenge.

One timid little boy hung back while the others were jumping, obviously wanting to try, but too nervous to do so.

"Come on, Harry," his friends called. "It's easy!"

At last he *did* jump, but lost his nerve and landed in the water. No real harm was done, but he scrambled out the other side, wet and a bit tearful.

I don't suppose the boy had ever heard of David Lloyd George, but that great statesman once said something which would have been a help to Harry. "Don't be afraid to take a big step if one is indicated. You can't cross a chasm in two small jumps!"

THE FRIENDSHIP BOOK

WHEN Mrs Dulcie Pratt of Solihull was a little girl she was given an autograph album. She asked her mother to sign the very first page and she has never forgotten the verse her mother wrote there.

Mrs Pratt tells me it has often encouraged her when times have been difficult, and she hopes it may cheer others, too:

> *Learn to make the most of life,*
> * Lose no happy day,*
> *Life will never give you back*
> * Chances swept away;*
> *Leave no tender word unsaid,*
> * Love while life shall last,*
> *For the mill can never grind*
> * With water that is past.*

MRS ALLAN was suddenly widowed and her neighbour and friend, Mrs Jones, found she just couldn't bear to face her to express her sympathy. She kept putting it off, becoming more and more embarrassed and, if she saw Mrs Allan in the street, would cross to the other side, pretending she didn't see her.

One day, climbing on to the bus to go home, she saw Mrs Allan sitting on one of the aisle seats, with two heavy bags of shopping. On impulse, she put out her hand and squeezed her friend's shoulder as she passed.

They got off the bus together and she took one of Mrs Allan's heavy bags, and so the ice was broken. Next day a note came through her door, from Mrs Allan: "Your sympathetic gesture meant more than words."

SUMMER'S GLORY

SUNDAY—JUNE 12.

FEAR not, for I am with you.

Isaiah 41:10

MONDAY—JUNE 13.

DURING the centenary celebrations in Italy to mark the birth of the composer Verdi, a concert was held at which leading figures in the musical world were invited to take part. The famous Toscanini was to conduct as were some lesser-known names. One of these was asked his fee and rather arrogantly replied that he would be content with a lira more than Toscanini.

When later he opened the envelope given to him he found it contained a single lira! Toscanini, truly great man that he was, had regarded it as sufficient reward merely to conduct on this very special occasion as his own humble tribute to a master musician.

TUESDAY—JUNE 14.

I OVERHEARD a remark on the bus one afternoon:

"But then Mabel *enjoys* all these committee and charity works." It was said scathingly, as if Mabel's enjoyment somehow robbed her good deeds of any value they might have.

But what on earth is wrong with enjoying doing good? A cup of tea offered cheerfully, a visit made with obvious interest and friendliness, are surely of much greater benefit to both giver and receiver than the same things offered in an atmosphere of stern duty.

So let's go ahead trying to add to the sum total of human happiness, even if it does include our own.

THE FRIENDSHIP BOOK

OUR old friend Mary put down her book when we called upon her recently.

"What are you reading, Mary?" asked the Lady of the House.

"Oh," she said, "this is just one of my lazy books."

"Lazy books!" I said. "What are they?"

She smiled. "Well, you see, I like good solid reading sometimes, but there are other times when I feel I can't make the effort, so I take something light and easy and call it a 'lazy book'!"

What a good idea! Our minds can't always be at full stretch and there is nothing to be ashamed of in reading something light and relaxing. Reading is for entertainment as well as education!

TURNER was perhaps the greatest landscape painter that ever lived. His success stemmed from his disciplined observations. For hours at a time he would gaze at the white clouds that scudded over the blue, and though he appeared idle, he was learning to paint those wonderful effects for which he was acclaimed.

It is said that, when he was a student, he set off one morning with his classmates who were intent on sketching. Turner sat down by a pond while the others went on. When they returned in the evening, Turner was still sitting there, and every now and then would throw a pebble into the water.

"We have had a splendid day," they exclaimed. "We've filled our sketchbooks. What have *you* done?"

"Well," said the young Turner, "I have done one thing. I have found out exactly how water looks when you throw a stone into it."

THE FRIENDSHIP BOOK

"BELIEVE in yourself." I read that advice recently and I think they are three words worth remembering.

Many psychologists maintain that it is essential for everyone to feel a sense of his or her true worth. Surely this is even more important in these times of mass unemployment.

"When God makes a man he breaks the mould". That is a quotation to cherish when faced with a sense of failure. There is no other person like you in the whole world.

The famous American poet Walt Whitman wrote:

Stand tall, walk tall, think tall,
As a man thinks so he is.
I am larger than I thought.
I did not know I held so much goodness.

CALLING on my friend Jimmy Morgan the other day I was surprised to find him with his hands busy in a baking bowl. Thinking that perhaps his wife was ill and he was taking over the household chores, I asked if Lucy was well.

"Oh, yes," he said, "but I just had this sudden urge to make some pancakes. Never done such a thing in my life before, but, you know, I sometimes get these sudden whims!"

I couldn't help thinking, "Good for you, Jimmy!" Of course, there is bound to be planning and routine about a good deal of our life, but I think people like Jimmy who are subject to "sudden whims" must get a lot of fun out of life.

How about exercising a sudden whim today?

F

THE FRIENDSHIP BOOK

SEEK ye the Lord while he may be found, call ye upon him while he is near.   Isaiah 55:6

KATHLEEN had had a long spell in hospital, and the other day when I went to visit someone else there, I met Kathleen who was just leaving.

"Hello," I said. "Have you been back for a check-up?"

"Oh, no," she replied. "I'm working here now. I've joined the voluntary dinner-helpers on the wards. I come only once a week, but I felt it was a small way of saying thanks for all the help I received when I was a patient here."

A small way? Well, perhaps, but would that we could all find such a practical way of saying, "Thank you"!

THE late Carlos Romulo, one-time President of the United Nations General Assembly, stood only five feet four inches in his shoes, but this never gave him an inferiority complex. He used to say, "I'm glad that I'm a little fellow," arguing that his size gave him many unexpected advantages.

He once said, "I must confess that in my younger days I experimented with wearing built-up shoes, but they made me feel uncomfortable — not physically, but mentally. They made me feel I was trying to appear something I was not, so I threw the shoes away."

How important it is, while doing the very best we can, to accept ourselves, and to be ourselves.

G

THE FRIENDSHIP BOOK

I LEARNED an interesting fact recently about the House of Commons. Apparently, on either side, just in front of the front benches are two red lines. If a speaker puts his foot across the line on his side, the cry goes up from anyone who notices it: "Order!"

The point is that the distance between the two lines is the distance between two men with swords outstretched, point to point. Is this, I wonder the origin of the phrase, "Keep your distance"?

It's wise for all of us to keep on the right side of the "red line" which can lead to quarrels.

THE Japanese nori farmers always have a special place in their hearts for Kasserine-San as they affectionately call Dr Kathleen Drew.

Dr Drew was the daughter of a Quaker agricultural machinery manufacturer from Lancashire. She graduated in 1922 from Manchester University with a first class honours degree in Botany.

When she heard that nori — a type of seaweed which the Japanese love to eat — was becoming scarce, she decided to do something about it. Working hard for several years, she eventually found an easy and successful way of growing it.

To say thank you in their own way, the farmers erected a statue to Kathleen above the Bay of Shimabara, and each year on the anniversary of her death they hold a ceremony and place on it the cap and gown in which she graduated.

We can't all be remembered in such a colourful fashion, or do something so vital, but there are always others who need our help in however small a way. The deed may seem tiny; the result can be enormous.

THE FRIENDSHIP BOOK

"SOME people think you haven't lived if you haven't had a holiday in Peru, China or Australia," commented a friend recently. "We can't all afford to travel around the world, but I've had some marvellous outings and holidays in Britain."

That set me thinking. It does seem that if you confess to spending your holidays in the Yorkshire Dales, the Welsh Mountains or the Western Isles, some people seem to regard it as second-best.

Yet there are so many beauty spots to be enjoyed in Britain.

W.H. Hudson, the famous naturalist and author, wrote in "Afoot in England":

"In reality those scenes which have given me the greatest happiness, the images of which are most vivid and lasting . . . were discovered as it were, by chance, which I had not heard of, or else had heard of and forgotten, or which I had never expected to see."

For him, every journey was one of exploration.

I DON'T know who wrote this little verse, but it appeared in one of the autograph albums that were so much in vogue some years ago:

> *Sow a thought, reap an act;*
> *Sow an act, reap a habit;*
> *Sow a habit, reap a character;*
> *Sow a character, reap a destiny.*

Of course it is just another way of expressing the old proverb, "We reap what we sow". Undoubtedly the things we do, live on. It is a comforting thought that we can leave beautiful and happy memories.

SUNDAY—JUNE 26.

COME now, and let us reason together, saith the Lord: though your sins be as scarlet, they shall be as white as snow.

Isaiah 1:18

MONDAY—JUNE 27.

LOOK at the lives of most really successful people and you will find that they learned to take hard knocks and overcome great obstacles to achieve what they did.

In one of his books, Laurens Van der Post, the famous author, sailor and explorer, tells how a Japanese friend once taught him judo. He likened the principles of the art to those of life, for "as in life, you have first to learn how to fall before you can learn how to rise; first master the law of losing properly before you can be worthy of winning".

TUESDAY—JUNE 28.

OUR friend Mary does marvellous tapestry and it's fascinating to watch her working deftly with her needles and wool. She begins with just a plain piece of canvas, and as she proceeds, a thing of beauty grows. First a stem appears, then a leaf, and finally a crimson rose with velvet-like petals is revealed. All is order, neatness and precision.

But turn the masterpiece over and it's a different story: bright patches of wool mingle with dark. There seems no pattern, no purpose; just a mass of interwoven threads — nothing as it should be, just chaos and disorder.

Isn't life like that? To us it may often seem to lack a pattern. It's only in retrospect that we see the hand of the Picture-maker at work.

THE FRIENDSHIP BOOK

" HAVE a nice day!" called a friend as she left recently. Another Americanism we've picked up in this country, I thought — and I wondered if it really meant anything.

It depends on who utters it, of course, and if it's sincere or merely a rather casual comment lacking genuine concern.

Thinking on these lines brought to mind a lesser-known American saying. It advises: "Tomorrow is the start of your new life."

While the great American President, Abraham Lincoln, said, "I have simply tried to do what seemed best each day, as each day came."

That surely makes for a "nice" day.

THE late James Louis Garvin, for over 30 years the editor of "The Observer" newspaper, has been described as "one of the brightest stars in the history of British journalism".

Perhaps the secret of his success can be detected in something he said when, as a young man, he applied for his first newspaper job on the "Newcastle Daily Chronicle". The editor warned him, "Journalism is a life of drudgery", and Garvin replied, "Everything in the world depends on drudgery, sir; even Bach's music, and cathedrals."

He knew that nothing of any real value can be accomplished without a lot of very hard work. A great piece of music; a fine building; a successful career — none of these is possible without long hours — days even — of what can only be described as drudgery.

The one who will endure that happily and cheerfully is the one who will shine, like J.L. Garvin.

JULY

FRIDAY—JULY 1.

IT'S easy to harbour a grudge, to store up resentment against someone who has treated you badly. Not so easy to forgive and forget.

Forgiveness, however, brings its own precious reward, as the German novelist and humorist Jean-Paul Richter knew. He once wrote, "The heart that forgives an injury is like the perforated shell of a mussel, which closes its wound with a pearl".

SATURDAY—JULY 2.

ON a July night in 1984, disaster struck York's magnificent Minster. Fire, probably caused by lightning, swept through the South Transept causing the collapse of the roof and threatening the famous 16th century Rose Window made up of red and white roses commemorating the end of the Wars of the Roses when Henry VII married Elizabeth of York. In a few moments, hundreds of years of history were in danger, and though the damage was severe, the prompt and courageous efforts of firemen and cathedral staff prevented what might have been greater loss.

The morning after, Peter Addeyman of the York Archaeological Trust was among the ruins where people were already busy at work cleaning the building.

"What impresses me most," he said, "is the way people have been looking to the future and not to the tragedy of last night."

Not easy, of course, but what a difference it makes to life's disasters when we can take that attitude toward them.

THE FRIENDSHIP BOOK

A MERRY heart doeth good like a medicine, but a broken spirit drieth the bones. Proverbs 17:22

W*HO with a little cannot be content*
Endures an everlasting punishment.

I came across these words the other day in a book of quotations, and thought how wise they were.

We all know people who feel they must keep up with the Joneses. The people next door have a new car, so they must have one, too; the lady across the street has a microwave oven, so her neighbour must have one, and so it goes on. It is an everlasting punishment, because these things have to be paid for and that can lead to financial difficulties, worries and discontent.

We would all be well to remember another old saying: "A contented mind is a blessing kind".

I WAS interested to learn that, hidden underground in the centre of Heathrow airport, is a chapel dedicated to St George. It was built for Christians to share, and is available at all times for those wanting a place for rest, quiet and prayer. Not only that, though, for the chaplains will assist with any problems and needs of passengers that cannot be dealt with elsewhere. So there in the midst of that modern and bustling place, the Christian Church is able to reach out and relieve the needs and anxieties of all kinds of people. Surely a most worthwhile and appreciated project.

G

THE FRIENDSHIP BOOK

WEDNESDAY—JULY 6.

A LITTLE while ago, the Lady of the House and I were engaged in one of our favourite pursuits — browsing round a secondhand bookshop.

The owner had pinned some carefully-written cards round the wall bearing quotations about books and reading. Although I do a good deal of reading of one kind and another, there was one saying that struck me in a completely new way.

It was by a John Burroughs and this was his thought: "I go to books as a bee goes to the flower — for a nectar that I can make into my own honey."

We thought it was a delightful way of expressing the joy, pleasure — and learning — to be derived from our reading.

THURSDAY—JULY 7.

M R SMITH was always afraid that he was going to forget something important, so he kept a long list of things he had to remember to do. It was headed in capital letters: "I MUST REMEMBER TO — " and below he wrote such things as "Pay electricity bill. Mend gate. Buy weed killer."

Perhaps in principle it was a good idea, but he went too far and even included items such as "Clean shoes. Empty pedal pin. Cut hedge."

One day, when the list was about a yard long, Mrs Smith had an idea and she squeezed in at the top of the list: "Tell my wife I love her."

She might have chosen something else, perhaps "Smile" or "Stop worrying", but the lesson for all of us is that we should try to get our priorities right. Isn't it more important that we should remember be happy and make others happy than to remember to shake up the cushions or sweep the garden path?

H

THE FRIENDSHIP BOOK

THAT great conductor, Sir John Barbirolli, brought delight to millions of people through the magnificent performances of the orchestras he led.

He had the reputation of being a hard and demanding taskmaster, and certainly he sought perfection from those who played under his baton. But a member of one of his orchestras has written, "Off the podium, he was just one of the band". He mixed with the rest, exchanging jokes and anecdotes, travelling on tour in trains and motor coaches, always preferring to have a seat with his players rather than sit in a first-class carriage.

His biographer adds, "Nobody took liberties because of this; they responded to his friendship, humanity and interest."

An interesting sidelight indeed upon a great artiste.

DO you really count your blessings? It is easy to do so when you have youth, ambition, health, strength and all your faculties to boost your enjoyment of life. You tend then to take things for granted.

It's when the going gets harder as limbs grow weary and life's tempo slows down that it becomes more difficult. It needn't be! If you have your eyesight you can re-live those walks in the country and the hills by scanning old photographs and browsing through illustrated books. Even if you can no longer attend concerts or the theatre there are always the TV, radio and records. The seasons with their own special joys come round regularly, and companionship and friendship are not rationed. There is so much to be thankful for.

SUNDAY—JULY 10.

THE Lord careth for strangers: he defendeth the fatherless and widow.   Psalms 146:9

MONDAY—JULY 11.

TWO French generals who were of equal rank and had each served in the army for the same number of years, enlisting on the same day, had a dispute about who should first salute the other. It was a silly quarrel, but eventually it became so bitter that the Marshal of France was asked to make a decision on it.

He at once said, "The most courteous of the two should be the one to salute first."

On being told this, the two generals immediately saluted each other at precisely the same moment. The quarrel was over.

TUESDAY—JULY 12.

GEORGE WITHER, a 17th century poet, wrote many hundreds of hymns, though only one of them now seems to appear in my hymn book — "Come, O come, in pious lays", usually sung to the tune familiar with "Come, ye thankful people, come", at harvest time.

Among his now unknown hymns are those on subjects such as "The Presentation of Twins to the Organist", "The Bursting of a Kitchen Boiler", "For Cripples", "While Dressing", "For the Contentedly Married", and so on!

Rather quaint? Perhaps so, yet these hymns show that George Wither had the right idea about religion — namely, that it is not just concerned with church and Sunday, but with all the ordinary events of everyday life.

THE FRIENDSHIP BOOK

WE have all heard the saying, "Schooldays are the happiest days of your life", though probably each of us has our own reaction to that.

I was amused by a comment a friend of mine made during a conversation on this subject. "Yes, they are the happiest days," he said, " — providing your children are old enough to go to school!"

CHARLIE came to garden for neighbours of ours many years ago when they were new to the area. He'd just retired from a lifetime's work on the railway, and unyielding tidiness was his rule. Our friends' garden didn't offer much in that line with an overgrown apple tree, bluebells rampaging everywhere, and two cats digging holes and damaging plants. However, Charlie eventually had everything straightened out to his liking, and colourful order prevailed, though over the years he frequently complained about interference from the cats.

"Them other gardeners," he would call them. "I can't stand 'em!" he would say, and the reasons for his animosity would follow at length.

Time passed and Charlie grew too old for gardening. He still visits our neighbours, however, and enjoys a cuppa, very often with "them other gardeners" in attendance. One morning, sitting stroking the elderly cat which was purring comfortably on his knees, he said to it with a chuckle, "You was my worst enemy, you was, and look at us now — the best of friends!"

Time had healed old sores, and Charlie had learned that often difficult lesson, to live and let live. I'm sure he felt a lot the better for it!

VILLAGE IDYLL

Timeless the scenes recalled with affection;
Why change a pattern close to perfection?

THE FRIENDSHIP BOOK

A COUPLE in York make regular visits to the grave of their daughter. Deanne was only 14 when she died. She had been physically handicapped from birth, yet throughout her short life, her happy personality and loving ways were an inspiration and joy to all who knew her.

Tragic? Undoubtedly. Although her mother admits to feeling shattered when Deanne died, she now believes that a great deal of good has resulted from her daughter's brief life. As she told me recently, she believes that everything in our lives does eventually work out to our ultimate good.

Deanne's parents have discovered tremendous joy in aiding other handicapped children in very many ways, and in helping their families to cope.

Deanne did not live in vain.

A FRIEND who was walking round my garden with me stopped to admire our display of Canterbury Bells. "Do you know how these flowers got their name, Francis?" he enquired.

I confessed I didn't, and he went on to explain how, in medieval times, pilgrims could buy, at many shrines, tiny bells to hang on horses' harnesses. Their tinkling sound would cheer the traveller on weary and sometimes dangerous stretches of road, and would also indicate to others the shrines that had been visited (rather like modern car window stickers!) It was from the Canterbury examples that our popular flowers got their name.

I have always been fond of Canterbury Bells, but they will bring fresh cheer to me now I know something of their fascinating history.

THE FRIENDSHIP BOOK

THY word is a lantern unto my feet, and a light unto my paths.   Psalms 119:105

CARL GUSTAV JUNG, the eminent psychiatrist, was once asked by a newspaper reporter if he believed God existed. When the interview was published, he was quoted as replying, "I do not believe I know."

In fact, what he had said was, "I do not believe — I know!"

A printer's error had completely changed the meaning of his reply.

How little it takes to twist or distort even the most definite and direct of statements!

HERE is a poem called "Contentment" sent to me by the poet Mary M. Milne:

What needs I with travel to Eastways or West,
Contentment is here with these things
I love best:
Logs burning brightly to crackle and spit,
Books on my table, of humour and wit.
Warm, fluffy slippers,
Fresh scones for tea,
Old cronies chin-wagging
With Floss at my knee;
Sunrise in the morning,
The air crisp and clear,
Why, what gain I from roving when my
* heart's right here!*

THE FRIENDSHIP BOOK

AT a table next to us in a small harbourside café were three elderly fishermen in deep discussion. The topic was friendship and the qualities which made a true friend.

It was interesting to hear the stories of kindly acts. They painted a clear picture of the closely-knit community in which the men lived.

Then one old man brought the discussion to an abrupt and thoughtful end by saying, with a twinkle in his eye: "To my mind a true friend is someone who knows all about you — but likes you all the same!"

"YOU couldn't possibly write a story as good as 'Treasure Island'!" jeered a young man at his brother, who was trying hard to become a successful author.

Oh, he couldn't, couldn't he? He'd show them! Rider Haggard called up all his resolution and plotting ability. The result was "King Solomon's Mines" — a book good enough to cause a sensation in the 19th century literary world both here and in America.

Had it not been for his brother's challenge, Rider Haggard might have gone on paddling in the shallows of authorship. Instead, he launched into the depths of adventure and it brought success.

The Cardiff-born novelist, Howard Spring, wrote in his autobiography: "There are times when, if a man is to be moved, he must be taken by the scruff of the neck, hustled out of his greenhouse and dumped into cold water."

I'm sure this statement refers to more than writing novels. Most of us need a push at some time to get on with what we should be doing.

THE FRIENDSHIP BOOK

"CAN you help me with my homework, Dad?" Young Joanna came up with the well-known plea, and Dad went over to see what he could do.

He looked at the maths book, but all the x's and y's and funny shapes meant nothing to him. Languages? He could still remember a smattering of French, but Joanna was doing German. He had to admit he was stumped.

Surely he could help with geography — that couldn't change. One look at the atlas told him different; he didn't know Brunei from Botswana.

So Dad tip-toed out to the kitchen, and five minutes later brought Joanna a hot cup of tea, a big slice of cake and a plateful of sandwiches.

"Gosh, thanks, Dad," said Joanna, as she tucked into her snack, and then started writing with twice as much determination as before.

Dad smiled quietly to himself. Yes, there was more than one way to help with homework!

A GOOD friend occasionally sends me a copy of her church magazine. An issue a little while ago contained the following anonymous verse which has some good advice for us all:

> One word won't tell folk who you are —
>   You've got to keep on talking;
> One step won't take you very far —
>   You've got to keep on walking;
> One inch won't make you very tall —
>   You've got to keep on growing;
> One trip to church won't tell you all —
>   You've got to keep on going.

THE FRIENDSHIP BOOK

BLESSED be he that cometh in the Name of the Lord: we have wished you good luck, ye that are in the house of the Lord. Psalms 118:26

DR. LUTHER EMMETT HOLT was a consultant in an American hospital for sick children. A nurse who worked with him told how he would often write on a child's chart, "This baby needs loving every three hours."

An unusual prescription, perhaps — but isn't it true that love is a remedy for countless of the world's ills? One of the greatest sources of happiness is in loving and being loved.

WHEN the Lady of the House and I were on holiday in Cheshire we visited the lovely National Trust property, Tatton Park, and were intrigued by a number of large ornamental stone urns on the top of a high garden wall. We couldn't help wondering why they were not filled with flowers, which would have made them look even more attractive.

When we made enquiries about this we discovered that they are not flower pots, but chimney pots! They stand on the top of wall flues and in the early Spring when there is still a danger of frost, fires are lit to keep the walls warm and thus protect the peach trees growing against them.

What a lovely idea! Things don't need to be ugly in order to be useful. Would that more thought were given in our world to utility *and* beauty!

THE FRIENDSHIP BOOK

YOU probably know the old joke about the man who was banging his head on the floor. When he was asked why he was doing it, he replied, "Because it's so nice when I stop!"

That's not really as silly as it sounds.

If we didn't work we could never enjoy holidays. We appreciate joys all the more when we have experienced sorrow. Would Spring be as delightful if we had not endured the Winter? It's good to remember when life is buffeting us how nice it will be when it stops!

AN immensely popular book last century was "The Scarlet Letter" by the American writer, Nathaniel Hawthorne. How it came to be written is a good example of how opportunities can be snatched at even the worst times.

Hawthorne lost his job as a customs officer and returned home deeply depressed, saying to his wife, "I am a complete failure." To his astonishment, instead of sharing his depression, she seemed overjoyed. "Now at last," she said, "you will have time to get on with the book you've been longing to write."

"How will we live in the meantime?" he protested.

Mrs Hawthorne unlocked a cupboard and brought out a large bag of money. "There is sufficient here for a whole year," she said. "I've always known you had it in you to write a great book, so every week I have been putting aside a little money for just such an opportunity."

"The Scarlet Letter" was written, owing much, not only to Nathaniel's genius, but also to Sophia Hawthorne's foresight and faith in her husband.

OF all the figures of fun created by Charles Dickens none is more memorable than Mr Micawber. Pompous and ostentatious, never a penny in his pocket, forever giving advice he couldn't follow, successful only in cutting a ridiculous figure as he tried hard to deceive himself, and others, that "Someday, something would turn up."

Mr Micawber's fate was to be forced by penury into aiding the rascally villain, Uriah Heep.

The great thing about Wilkins Micawber was that in the end something *did* turn up. He recovered his dignity, at the risk of losing all, by denouncing Heep. A changed man, Micawber headed for Australia and, hopefully, a better life.

Just one brave action can sometimes save a tawdry existence. Those who wait with patience and optimism for their lives to change are not always doomed to disappointment. There *can* be light at the end of the tunnel.

SATURDAY—JULY 30.

WE are all familiar with the old adage, "Never put off till tomorrow what you can do today", and no doubt we recognise its wisdom if we do not always follow the advice.

Recently, on a church Wayside Pulpit noticeboard, I came across a rather different, but perhaps even more important injunction: "It is well to put off till tomorrow what you ought not to do at all"!

SUNDAY—JULY 31.

FOR God is the King of all the earth: sing ye praises with understanding. Psalms 47:7

AUGUST

MONDAY—AUGUST 1.

THE Northumberland poet, Margaret Riley, wrote these lines about being alone. I think they express what most people feel, especially older folk:

> *I'm not afraid to be alone,*
> *It doesn't bother me;*
> *It gives me time to sit and think,*
> *To let my thoughts go free.*
>
> *I like to plan the days ahead,*
> *Recall events long past,*
> *To wonder what the future holds*
> *— Time goes so very fast.*
>
> *I may not finish all I plan,*
> *I know I often stray;*
> *When memories of youth intrude,*
> *There's no work done that day.*
>
> *I think of friends from long ago*
> *I very seldom see.*
> *No, I'm not lonely by myself,*
> *My thoughts are company.*

TUESDAY—AUGUST 2.

"MR GAY," said little Billy to me the other day. "What did the policeman say to the three angels?"

"I don't know, Billy." I replied, "but I'm sure you're going to tell me!"

Billy bent his knees three times like a traditional policeman and said, "Halo, halo, halo!"

THE FRIENDSHIP BOOK

A FRIEND in America occasionally sends me a young people's magazine, the back page of which is devoted to short sayings sent in by readers. Here are a few of them:

"If your mind should go blank, don't forget to turn off the sound."

"Forbidden fruit is responsible for many a bad jam."

"A pessimist is a person who is always blowing out the light to see how dark it is."

"An easy conscience makes a soft pillow."

" IT'S just that I'm getting older," an 80-year-old man said to me after apologising for not climbing nimbly on the village bus, "but I do hope I never grow crabby with it."

On the journey he told me that towards the end of his working life as a male nurse, he had spent several years in an old people's home.

"Do you know," he said, "I noticed that those old folk who retained their interest in life, in the things going on in the outside world and in the others round about them, seemed to keep their mental faculties sharper than the ones who were self-centred. It makes you think."

It does indeed. There is no doubt that the best way to enjoy the later years of life is to remember that there's always something to look forward to and something interesting to see.

The great Leonardo da Vinci wrote in one of his notebooks: "Iron rusts from disuse; stagnant water loses its purity, and in cold weather becomes frozen; even so does inaction sap the vigour of the mind."

Worth remembering, whatever age you are.

THE FRIENDSHIP BOOK

AN elderly lady had achieved fame as an artist rather late in life. At the opening of an exhibition of her work, she was being interviewed by a young art critic.

It was well known that she had had many problems and tragedies during her life and the critic remarked that none of her paintings seemed to reflect those difficult times, but were all bright and cheerful. Why was this so?

"The art of life," she replied simply, "is using the shadows to emphasise the highlights."

THE first Saturday in August is special in the ancient town of Ripon in Yorkshire. It is St Wilfred's Day when a man, dressed as a Bishop, rides a white horse through the market place and streets to the Cathedral to commemorate the return of Bishop Wilfred hundreds of years ago. Nowadays he leads a colourful procession of decorated floats.

Wilfred was one of the great 7th century English Christians. He came to Ripon and erected a monastery on the foundations of one originally built by the monks of Melrose Abbey. Later he became Bishop, but was put into prison by Archbishop Theodore for daring to appeal to Rome against an unjust rule.

On his release and return to Ripon, he rode triumphantly through the district, enthusiastically greeted by faithful crowds.

In 672, he built his first church at Ripon and dedicated it to St Peter. The present, much later Cathedral is dedicated to St Peter and St Wilfred. Only the tiny crypt remains of St Wilfred's Church, with its opening known as "St Wilfred's Needle", but the memory of a good and courageous man lives on.

H

THE FRIENDSHIP BOOK

BLESSED be the Lord God of Israel; for he hath visited and redeemed his people.   Luke 1:68

MONDAY—AUGUST 8.

WHEN our Sunday School held its anniversary service, we had a splendid sermon. However, I'm sure the preacher wouldn't mind my saying that the two most impressive parts were, firstly, when a group of about 20 Sunday School teachers joined in a simple act of re-dedication to their work, and secondly, when a choir of over 100 children sang, "O Jesus, I have promised to serve thee to the end."

All of which reminds me of J. Arthur Rank. Rank was a wealthy flour miller, and a film magnate, who had influence, riches and fame; but he was also a Methodist Sunday School teacher and he once said, "Nothing gives me more consolation and satisfaction than my work in the Sunday School."

I remembered that when I listened to our Sunday School teachers and their children, and I thanked God for them.

TUESDAY—AUGUST 9.

I LIKE this simple and beautiful verse by Joyce Frances Carpenter, of Holland Park in London:

The perfume of the wind-blown flowers,
*   The glowing warmth of Summer sun,*
A little kindness from a friend,
*   The daily loaf; some work well done.*
My slippers when my feet feel tired,
*   A favourite book, some music gay,*
The knowledge that God's arms are near!
*   These things have brought me joy today.*

THE FRIENDSHIP BOOK

MY friend Raymond gently put me in my place the other evening. We were walking home together on one of the most beautiful starlight nights I remember for some time. In fact, we stopped for several minutes to gaze in wonder at the star-studded sky.

At last I said, "Doesn't it make you feel insignificant?"

Raymond paused for a moment before answering, and then he said quietly, "Well, no, it doesn't really, Francis. It makes me proud and glad to be part of such a wonderful universe!"

A good way of looking at it, don't you think?

HOLIDAYMAKERS to North Yorkshire will probably have visited the hand-made furniture workshop of the late Robert Thompson, known as "the Mouseman" because of the tiny mouse he carved on every piece of furniture he made.

He was a craftsman of the highest order and demanded of those who worked for him the standards he imposed upon himself.

His English oak was thoroughly seasoned for three to five years before he considered it fit to use. Only once had he to buy some oak from another country which he used to make some chairs for a Scarborough family. It was Irish bog oak, and he must have been dissatisfied with them, for some years later he asked the family to sell the chairs back to him as he couldn't bear to think of them bearing his trademark.

We can't all be Robert Thompsons, but we won't go far wrong if we live by the motto: "Only the best is good enough".

THE FRIENDSHIP BOOK

WHAT a good friend a dog can be! Margaret Riley, from near Wooler, Northumberland, wrote these charming lines about a Border collie:

> Were you really that maddening pup
>   Who rampaged through our home?
> You chased the cat and chewed my boots,
>   You even ate a comb.
>
> And then you started training hard,
>   Your puppy days were past.
> You learned to sit, to find and fetch,
>   You grew up very fast.
>
> With head held high, eyes alert,
>   You waited for commands
> To help and find lost lambs and sheep
>   Amongst these rough moorlands.
>
> Just now you're lying warm and snug
>   With a basket and a bone,
> You're busier than you've ever been
>   With four pups of your own!

THE new vicar was paying a first call on one of his parishioners.

"I understand," he said to the old man, "that you're the only person in the parish who can tell the correct time by the church clock."

"That's right," came the answer. "When the hands of that clock stand at 12, then it strikes two."

"But which is right?" asked the bewildered clergyman.

"Neither — it's 20 minutes to seven!"

THE PRESENCE

*There's more to an island paradise
Than sand no foot has trod.*

Listen, for through the silence
Can be heard the voice of God.

THE FRIENDSHIP BOOK

SEARCH the scriptures; for in them ye think ye have eternal life: and they are they which testify me.
                                                            John 5:39

THE word "friend" is often loosely used. Sometimes we speak of a neighbour or even the merest acquaintance as a friend. Of course, there are pleasant neighbours and agreeable acquaintances, but ought there not to be something very special about a friend?

I like the definition I heard many years ago which makes this distinction between a neighbour and a friend: "Neighbourliness *looks* over the fence; friendship *goes* over it."

MARTIN was a tonic to all who knew him — full of laughter and humour and able to converse upon most topics. "Life is fascinating," he would say. Yet when the Lady of the House and I first met him, he had been an invalid for 30 years and in hospital for the last eight.

Since his youth, he had been unable to go out and meet the world and so he had invited it to come to him, and spent much of his time reading books and newspapers.

Despite his disabilities he was always ready to try his hand at painting, weaving, pottery and whatever else he could — and then to give away his work for others to enjoy.

No wonder he found life so full of interest — he never gave himself time to do anything else.

THE FRIENDSHIP BOOK

HAVE you noticed that, long after a holiday, the things you remember about it are often quite small incidents? It's hard to say why, but holiday photographs and souvenirs seldom invoke as vivid memories for us as some small happening which seemed trivial at the time.

I wonder what, if anything, we shall remember about today in a year or so. Perhaps it will be a chance meeting with someone, a friendly smile or a kindly word. Who knows? It's certainly wise to treasure each good thing that makes up today — it could be next year's memory!

IN different parts of Britain there are reminders of how much we owe to animals and how we should treat them.

One of these is a horse trough at the top of Wharf Brow, near Pewsey in Wiltshire. It was erected many years ago by Jonathan Puckridge, a former London grocer who retired to Pewsey. He loved nothing better then exploring the district in a horse-drawn carriage. Whenever he drove out of Pewsey he always allowed his horse to rest before beginning the steep rise of Wharf Brow. At the top, he erected the horse trough with these words engraved on it:

A man of kindness to his horse is kind,
A brutish action shows a brutal mind,
Remember, He who made thee, made the brute,
He can't complain, but God's all-seeing eye
Beholds thy cruelty and hears his cry,
He was designed thy servant, not thy drudge,
Remember His Creator is thy Judge.

REGATTA DAY

THE FRIENDSHIP BOOK

I LIKE the sentence from a Sikh prayer which says, "You, Lord, are near, yet we climb a palm tree to see you!"

God, love, beauty, friendship, happiness, peace, contentment — what strenuous efforts we make sometimes to achieve these experiences when, if we would only be still and look about us, we should find they were close at hand all the time!

YEARS ago, at a seaside holiday resort, I met two dear old ladies who insisted that they derived great benefit from what they called their "daily paddle". Yet they merely strolled along the sands at the very edge of the water, just allowing the tide to tickle their toes!

I wonder if we aren't sometimes a bit like that in life.

In her autobiography, the poet and author, Patience Strong, tells that the novelist Neil Bell once advised her "Don't paddle in the shallows of life".

Jesus advised, indeed ordered, his disciples to "Launch out into the deeps and let down your nets for a draught". His advice did not apply only to fishing. Nor does it mean only "paddling".

It means don't be content with what you can do easily — try something harder, something you've always wanted to do, but didn't dare in case of failure. To fail is surely better than never to try.

In the modern phrase, "stretch" yourself, and not only in physical exercise. Many handicapped people have proved successful in the way they have dared to attempt some challenging feat. Surely we more fortunate people can imitate them in this?

THE FRIENDSHIP BOOK

AND Jesus said unto them, I am the bread of life: he that cometh to me shall never hunger; and he that believeth on me shall never thirst.   John 6:35

I AM told there was once an inn in Cheltenham with the unusual name of The Five Alls.

On its sign were pictures of five people: a king whose motto was "I rule for all"; a bishop whose motto was "I pray for all"; a lawyer whose motto was "I plead for all"; a soldier whose motto was "I fight for all"; and a workman whose motto was "I work for all".

Notice that all five were from different stations in life, but had one thing in common — they were working for the good of others. A happy band indeed!

ALTHOUGH Charles Reade, the 19th century author, wrote many books denouncing the social evils of his day, most of them have been forgotten and he is remembered mainly for his novel "The Cloister and the Hearth".

Even so, I wonder how many people are familiar with the opening words of that book. They are, "Not a day passes over the earth but men and women of no note do great deeds, speak great words, and suffer noble sorrows."

It reminds me of a verse I heard long ago:

The world may sing of its gallant brave
And their names may resplendent shine,
But the heroes the world has never known
Shall be crowned with a love divine.

THE FRIENDSHIP BOOK

J. M. ROBERTSON of Edinburgh sent me this amusing poem about the wildlife in his garden. It's called "The Intruders":

> Don't think I am complaining,
>   But each tell-tale sign suggests
> My garden is a haven
>   For some uninvited guests . . .
>
> There's the energetic squirrel,
>   See him scrape for this and that;
> By his very speed of movement,
>   He infuriates the cat.
>
> There are blue-tits, there are blackbirds,
>   There are sparrows by the score,
> All seeking crumbs of comfort
>   In each picking, pecking chore.
>
> The hedgehog realises
>   Sheer endeavour cannot fail,
> And with that extra effort,
>   He can overtake the snail.
>
> Considering the pleasures
>   These intruders bring to me,
> I really have no option
>   But to let them live rent-free!

THERE are many sayings about happiness, but here is one new to me:
The time to be happy is now.
The place to be happy is here.
The way to be happy is to make others so.

STABLE GIRL

*Come over here! I'll let you see
A friend who's all the world to me.*

THE FRIENDSHIP BOOK

I HEARD the other day of a glamorous film star who bruised her leg whilst travelling on board an ocean liner.

The purser sent out an appeal for a doctor and a man came forward. However, when he questioned him, the purser found he was not a doctor of Medicine but of Law.

"She won't know the difference," said the man and he hurried to the film star's cabin, only to find that he had been beaten to it — by a doctor of Divinity!

ALTHOUGH we all know that we alter the clocks in Spring and Autumn, it's still easy to forget when they go forward and when they go back. However, if we remember that the Americans speak of Autumn as the "Fall" there is a simple way of remembering what to do with the clocks — "Spring forward — fall back!"

When you think about it, this business of "forward" and "backward" is to do with more than the clocks. It is to do with life. We have a good friend who must have helped scores of people by her quiet kindliness. She simply tells them, "Remember, I am always here if you want me." Then she seems to fall into the background, but is always ready to spring forward as soon as she can be of help.

To know when to draw backward and when to spring forward is the very nature of true helpfulness.

I F ye love me, keep my commandments.

John 14:15

THE FRIENDSHIP BOOK

MONDAY—AUGUST 29.

I LIKE the story about three-year-old Thomas who had been taught to take care of other people's property.

One day, whilst visiting his grandmother, he spilled his orange juice in the garden. Running inside, he returned with a cloth explaining, "Nana won't want her grass spoilt!"

TUESDAY—AUGUST 30.

ONE Sunday when staying with a friend I went with him to his local church. During the service the vicar rose to introduce the Dean who was visiting the parish and was to preach the sermon. The vicar's words of introduction were long and elaborate, listing the Dean's achievements in a rather embarrassing way.

At last the vicar stopped and the Dean walked to the pulpit to begin his sermon. Before doing so, however, he turned to the vicar and said, "Thank you. After an introduction like that I can hardly wait to hear what I've got to say!"

WEDNESDAY—AUGUST 31.

GEORGE MIKES, the Hungarian writer, tells in one of his books of a wealthy couple he knew who lived on the French Riviera. A superb place to live? Not really, for they could never go out together. One always had to stay at home to keep an eye on their Picasso and Monet paintings in case they were stolen.

Mikes asks, "What belonged to whom? Did the pictures belong to them, or did they belong to the pictures?"

Their possessions were not a pleasure to them, but a burden and a source of continual fear and anxiety.

SEPTEMBER

THURSDAY—SEPTEMBER 1.

NOTHING is more delightful than the simple candour of children. I'm sure no parents have ever escaped a blush or two because of their outspoken offspring.

Tommy was at a children's party and was asked by his hostess if he would like more jelly.

"Yes, please," replied Tommy. "Mum said I wasn't to ask for a second helping — but she didn't know how small the first helpings were going to be!"

FRIDAY—SEPTEMBER 2.

"INTERESTING, isn't it?" remarked the artist as he skilfully pencilled in lines that gradually transformed his blank sketch-pad into a flowing landscape of beautiful shades. "These railway lines converge — and yet they never meet!" He could, of course, have been talking about everything in his picture, for his careful perspective took the lines of the stone bridge, the rickety fence, the clumps of trees, and so on, far away into the distance, to his unseen vanishing point.

In reality, one of a pair of railway lines would be absolutely useless without the other, but placed, untouching, side by side, they carry people and goods efficiently (usually!) to their various destinations.

Similarly, we travel through life without meeting thousands of other human beings upon whom we depend for our needs and small luxuries. Our journeys are in parallel, too, and we, and our fellow passengers and helpers, travel ever onward towards perfection and to that mutual focal point.

ACHIEVEMENT

THE FRIENDSHIP BOOK

B ETTY is an elderly lady who lives alone, but who tells me that she always has plenty of company. How? Well, for years she has cultivated the art of letter writing. Through her correspondence she keeps in constant touch with distant relatives; she has traced old school friends and regularly drops them a line — to which they always respond with bits of their news. Friendships made on holiday over the years have been cemented this way, too.

"What on earth do you find to write about?" she is often asked. She replies that she finds it easy, just by following a bit of advice given to someone by the author, Evelyn Waugh: "Write as if you were talking to me. A letter should be a form of conversation."

Betty confirms the opinion of Lord Byron: "Letter writing is the only device for combining solitude and good company."

C OUNSEL in the heart of man is like deep water, but a man of understanding will draw it out.

Proverbs 20:5

A T the end of the 18th and beginning of the 19th century, a clergyman, the Rev. Sydney Smith, earned a reputation as a writer and wit.

He had great skill in deflating the pompous, but he also had a gentle heart, and some of his remarks must have brought comfort to many. I particularly like the encouragement given in these words, "It is the greatest of all mistakes to do nothing because you can do only a little."

K

THE FRIENDSHIP BOOK

I WAS helping a group to collect on a charity flag day. We split into pairs and spread out along the busier streets of the town centre.

During a lull in the flow of shoppers passing our corner, I was chatting with my partner, who's blind. Suddenly he asked me why I had let some people pass by without approaching them with my collecting tin. I could only answer that I supposed they didn't look as if they would be very sympathetic.

"I thought so," he said. "I don't have that problem. As far as I'm concerned every pair of feet belongs to a human being."

After that, I felt that I had to approach everyone who came along — and I was surprised how many of the "unsympathetic" ones smiled and gave a donation.

Appearances can be very deceptive.

L AURA loved to walk in fields and gardens where she could admire beauty, colour and scents. She never went to college, yet she became a designer. Her first printed designs were done on the kitchen table, with her husband's help. They were for a pretty apron and gardening overall covered with sprigs of wild flowers and leaves. These dainty floral designs, and many others that Laura continued to produce, soon became known all over the world. Laura and her husband had started a business which just grew and grew, and the name Laura Ashley became world-famous.

Sadly, in 1985, Laura had an accident and died. A friend said simply, "She's not gone, we think of her every day." How could we forget the lady whose little blue flowers look at us and say "Forget-me-not"?

THE FRIENDSHIP BOOK

IN one of his books, the American preacher, Dr R.J. McCracken, tells of an old countryman, a devout Methodist, who, when he heard the sound of the angelus bell from a Roman Catholic chapel in the neighbouring village, took off his hat, stood for a moment in silence, and then said, "In my Father's House are many mansions."

How much happier a place the world would be, not only in the realm of religion, but in much else besides, if we could cultivate in ourselves that spirit of tolerance.

NOT many people come home chuckling from a visit to the dentist, but the Lady of the House did just that.

Peter had been telling her about the holiday from which he and his family had just returned. They had got a great bargain of a vase, just perfect for his wife's flower arranging. Then, just as he was unloading the car when they got home — disaster! The vase fell out of its wrapping and shattered.

The wife was very upset and said so! While all poor Peter could do was pick up the pieces, put them in the bin and say again how sorry he was. They agreed she would say no more about it.

"And of course she's kept her word?" said the Lady of the House.

"Yes, she's never mentioned it. But I notice that whenever someone asks us about our holiday she will say: 'Oh, we'd a super time. Of course we had a little disaster, but I'll leave Peter to tell you about that!'"

Trust a woman to get her own back in the nicest possible way!

AUTUMN MAJESTY

THE FRIENDSHIP BOOK

BEFORE Dr Johnson became famous through the publication of his great dictionary, he and his wife, Tetty, were often pushed to make ends meet. Johnson would grumble about the meals she served, till one day she could stand his complaining no longer and just as Johnson was about to say grace, she held up her hand.

"Wait," she said, "let us not make a farce of asking a blessing on a meal which you will shortly declare uneatable."

I'm sure that Johnson, who was by nature a kindly man, got the message.

AND all the people then shouted, and said, Great is Truth, and mighty above all things.   I Esdras 4:41

A CHURCH council was alarmed to hear that it would cost over £200 for some dead elms to be cut down on the churchyard boundary. Then one of the council members said quietly, "Leave it to me."

Ken Hutchings may never preach a sermon or even read a lesson in church, but he uses other gifts. In a few days he had not only cut down the elms but sawn up the timber and sold the logs. So instead of receiving a hefty bill, the churchyard fund found itself £52 better off. Not surprisingly, someone was heard to comment, "Ken is a great feller!"

Many different skills are needed in every community. No one person possesses them all. Sooner or later something needs doing which will be "just up our street." Then we, too, can say, "Leave it to me."

THE FRIENDSHIP BOOK

"WHAT a lovely day we had, and wasn't the sunset beautiful!" I remarked to our caterer-in-chief on the way home from our church picnic at the seaside.

"I was much too busy with arrangements and refreshments to enjoy anything, and I certainly didn't notice any sunset," was the somewhat tart response.

I sighed. Poor Mrs Wilson! No matter how many people combine to help her, she is forever fussing about the next move. This time it had been about where we should all sit and how the food should be served. Then immediately the picnic was over, it was about the packing up and the details of the journey home.

There are far too many Mrs Wilsons in the world, worthy souls, but always anxiously preparing for the next step, missing out entirely on the best things along life's way.

SHARON called out to her mother after being put to bed to sleep, and knowing her daughter's little ways, Mother went upstairs armed with a glass of water, for this was usually what was wanted.

"Not asleep yet?" she asked.

"I've been thinking," said Sharon. "Telling a lie is a worse thing than stealing, isn't it?"

Her mother looked surprised. "Why do you think lying is worse than stealing?"

"Well," Sharon replied, "if you steal something, you can take it back, or if you have eaten it, you could pay for it, but a lie is for always."

A profound thought — at bedtime or any other time.

THE FRIENDSHIP BOOK

THE late Lord Brabazon of Tara had some very wise advice for those who tend to worry about the future — whether their own or that of the world in which we live. He said in a radio broadcast: "If you can train yourself not to worry, you will have done more for yourself than any doctor can do. The unpleasant things in my life have always happened out of the blue. Meetings and other events I have dreaded and feared like the plague have turned out not to be so bad. Do not hide today's sun behind tomorrow's clouds."

ANYONE who has had the blessings of a dog's companionship will realise the truth of the description a "faithful friend", yet few experience the kind of tactful help that the poet William Wordsworth had from his Lakeland terrier. Wordsworth enjoyed long walks with his dog, and on these he would mull over ideas for a verse, or speak aloud some completed ones.

Sometimes visitors to the Lake District would pass the tall man who seemed to be talking to himself. It was all very well for his master to talk away when there was nobody about, but he really should shut up when strangers approached. So, as Wordsworth relates in "The Prelude", the terrier trotted on in front:

> *. . . but when ere he met*
> *A passenger approaching he would turn*
> *To give me timely notice and straight way*
> *Grateful for that admonishment I hushed*
> *My voice, composed my gait . . .*

A faithful friend indeed!

THE FRIENDSHIP BOOK

I WAS sitting on a grassy bank, enjoying the sunshine and watching a bumble bee going from flower to flower. I was joined by 12-year-old Graham and we sat without speaking for a while, watching and listening to the bumble bee. Then Graham spoke:

"Did you know, Mr Gay, that a bumble bee has no right to be flying at all?"

"What do you mean?" I asked.

"Well," said Graham seriously, "I was reading in a book just yesterday that according to the laws of flight a bumble bee shouldn't be able to fly because its body is too heavy and its wings too short."

"Really?" I said, waiting for him to go on. He was quiet for a minute, then he added, "Isn't it a good thing bumble bees don't read books!"

FOR God so loved the world, that he gave his only begotten Son, that whosoever believeth in him should not perish, but have everlasting life.   John 3:16

THE famous wildlife artist, David Shepherd, gave a demonstration of painting on television, and as he completed the picture he said, "Well, that's it, I think. Not that I'm really satisfied with it. I am *never* satisfied. When you're satisfied you make no progress."

That's true of more than painting. As Robert Browning said,

Ah, but a man's reach should exceed his grasp,
Or what's a heaven for?

BY AVON

The tallest spire in England
Soars above Avon's banks;
A pleasant, restful place to sit,
And, quietly, give thanks.

THE FRIENDSHIP BOOK

IN one of A. E. W. Mason's novels an old sea-captain describes Nelson. "Yes, I've seen him," he says. "Nothing much to see! A little chap, light in the waist and thin as paper. Nothing to look at and mild as milk. One arm, one eye and about half a man, and as sick as a three months' old puppy when there's a heavy sea and weighs about as much as a ship's boy. But, in action, when the bulkheads are down and the linstocks lighted, then . . . "

"Yes?" said his companion.

"Then he is a flame of fire!"

We can't all be Nelsons, but if, when the moment arises, we can kindle a flame of enthusiasm or of love, of faith, or whatever the need of the hour, we, too, will cease to be merely "little chaps"!

HAVE you ever been blackberrying? I love to roam down country lanes, tub in hand, seeking out the dark, glistening fruit — brambles, they call them in Scotland. The best of them always seem to be that little bit out of reach and you have to stretch over to pluck them from the back of the prickly bush. Often, my arms get scratched by thorns and sometimes a few of the smaller berries in my punnet may roll away and be lost in the undergrowth. But it's always worth it to make the effort to reach the pick of the crop.

Life's like that, isn't it? The things really worth achieving are never easily won. Obstacles are always in the way and we may have to sacrifice something we hold dear for a higher goal. Passing a driving test, learning a language, or even gaining a university degree is never easy, but, oh, the satisfaction of winning through!

THE FRIENDSHIP BOOK

JEAN loves sewing and she often sits at a window looking down on Fred Smith's little corner shop. It's a very busy place with people going in and out every hour of the day.

"Do you know what I've noticed?" Jean said to me one day. "All sorts of people go into that shop, but no matter what they go in to buy they all come out smiling."

I was saying to myself what a pleasant thought this was when Jean added, "Of course Fred Smith is a very friendly man. He always has a cheerful word for everybody."

Smile, and the world smiles with you.

OVER 50 years ago, Matthew Kerr had a wonderful idea. He would build a miniature railway and all the thousands of children who came to spend a holiday at the seaside town of Arbroath would be able to enjoy the thrill of riding in a carriage pulled by a real engine.

Since then, generations of boys and girls, yes and grans and granpas, too, over 1½ million of them, have travelled on that track and got a wave and a toot of the whistle from the driver of the express thundering along, almost beside them, on the London-Aberdeen main line. All the "big" drivers have a soft spot for Matthew Kerr's railway.

In this world of spaceships perhaps Matthew's railway isn't very important. But when I think of that host of happy children I remember the words of the poet:

> He who gives a child a treat
> Makes joy-bells ring in heaven's street.

THE FRIENDSHIP BOOK

A COUPLE of hundred years ago, there were two Irish families in adjoining cottages who, for some long-forgotten reason, had fallen out. For years the feud had continued, with the families refusing to speak to one another.

One day, one of the fathers decided it had all gone on for long enough. There was a gap in the wall which separated the two cottages, and the man simply went up and thrust his arm through the gap. Then he waited. After a long pause, he felt a hand on the other side of the wall seize his and grasp it in friendship. The feud was over. It is said that this is how the phrase "to chance one's arm" passed into the language.

If only there were more people who were willing to "chance their arm". . .

F OR in him we live, and more, and have our being; as certain also of your poets have said, For we are also his offspring.   Acts 17:28

M ANY years ago, I copied into one of my notebooks these words from a magazine article by the American writer, Hal Borland: "If dawn only came once a year we would all gather on the hilltops to see it and celebrate; we would hold festivals and issue proclamations and utter prayers of thanksgiving."

Because this miracle of the morning occurs every day, we take it for granted. Just now and again, it is worth being up to greet the birth of a new day, a day that never was before, and to share in its freshness and its hope.

THE FRIENDSHIP BOOK

AN old lady I knew had a mind stored with simple sayings and verses which she loved to recite to us — and she seemed to have something appropriate for every occasion.

I remember one in particular which she would repeat if any of us tended to be worried or upset about anything. Quietly she would say,

> *Said the sparrow to the robin,*
> *"I should really like to know*
> *Why these anxious human beings*
> *Rush about and worry so."*
>
> *Said the robin to the sparrow,*
> *"Friend, I think that it must be*
> *That they have no heavenly Father*
> *Such as cares for you and me."*

KINDLY, gentle criticism can often be more effective than an angry reproach and it is the truly great men and women who seem best to understand and use this.

The cellist, Pablo Casals, was teaching a class of young musicians and found that one student had foolishly chosen a piece far beyond his abilities, probably trying to show off before the rest of the class. Of course, his performance was a disaster and the rest of the pupils held their breath, expecting Casals to tear the arrogant young man to pieces.

Instead, quietly he said, "That is a fine piece of music you have chosen and I congratulate you on your good taste. Now, let's go over the first part together."

Patiently he proceeded to help his pupil to correct his mistakes.

THE FRIENDSHIP BOOK

I WAS reading recently a book about the life and work of the great statesman, W. E. Gladstone. His biographer tells how, hanging over the head of Gladstone's bed was one of those framed texts, so popular in those days.

The words were from Isaiah: "Thou wilt keep him in perfect peace whose mind is stayed on Thee because he trusteth in Thee."

If someone caught up in the almost intolerable burdens of government, political controversy and decision-making found his strength in these words, we can surely do likewise.

A YOUNG friend was widowed after only a few years of marriage. With two small children to care for, she was often exhausted. Everything seemed so much effort.

After a few months she visited her husband's family, who lived in a small town straggling up a steep hillside. One day she was climbing back up the hill, pushing the baby and the shopping in the pram. The toddler, walking beside her, was getting tired and wanted to be carried, too. She stopped for a rest, thinking she would never get back to the house.

Just then, an old man stopped to pass the time of day. She commented on the difficulty of the climb. "Yes," he replied. "That's the good thing about these hills — there's always something to raise your eyes to!"

For the first time she looked beyond the houses to the distant fields and woods, and saw how beautiful the hills really were. Suddenly, the journey home didn't seem nearly so long or the hill so steep.

OCTOBER

"PROBLEMS can be endured if the sufferer has inner resources." That was the belief of one of Britain's most famous writers, Rudyard Kipling, who was born in Bombay on 30th December 1865.

The well-known author and winner of the Nobel Prize for Literature in 1907, had often to test this belief.

As a five-and-a-half year old boy sent from his parents in India because of the climate, he had been extremely unhappy for five years with a family at Southsea.

Sadly, his unhappiness continued in later life. Even after his marriage, he and his American-born wife needed fortitude again and again. When Kipling was gravely ill in South Africa, their young daughter Josephine died in 1899. In 1915, their only son, 18-year-old John, was reported missing after the Battle of Loos.

Kipling's own health was often poor. He suffered for years from undiscovered duodenal ulcers. He also needed courage in his career, for some critics sneered at his writing and called him an Imperialist because he was proud of Britain's role in the world.

Much of the renewal of their courage came to the Kiplings at Bateman's, Sussex, their tranquil home. This is now a National Trust property and visitors can see the study where Kipling worked and where he discovered so many inner resources for 33 years.

SO then faith cometh by hearing, and hearing by the word of God.   Romans 10:17

THE FRIENDSHIP BOOK

ACROSS the Atlantic and through our letter-box come regular letters from Anne Johnson, a pen friend of the Lady of the House. Her latest one contained these anonymous quotations, all about friendship:

"The best time to make friends is before you need them."

"A true friend laughs at your stories even when they're not so good, and sympathises with your troubles even when they're not so bad."

"The best way to keep friendships from breaking is not to drop them."

"When you've made a fool of yourself, a real friend doesn't believe you've done a permanent job."

"Friendship is like a bank account — you cannot draw upon it without making deposits."

I POPPED in to see my old friend Mary the other afternoon and we shared a pot of tea in her warm kitchen, still fragrant with the smell of freshly-baked loaves. As we chatted she told me how she enjoyed the leisurely process of making bread.

"Some people allow their dough to rise very quickly in a hot kitchen," said Mary, "but I always start mine in the evening and then it rises slowly, overnight, in a cold room. That way," she continued, "the bubbles of carbon dioxide spread evenly through the dough and the result is a beautifully textured loaf that never crumbles, unlike a quickly-risen dough that is so full of holes that the bread collapses in crumbs when it is cut."

Rather like life, isn't it? Patience is one of those qualities that usually works out best in the long run, whilst a hasty word or act can cause no end of trouble.

K

THE FRIENDSHIP BOOK

ONCE when George Washington was riding with friends, one of the horses kicked a few stones from the top of the wall it had leaped over.

"We'd better put those back," said Washington.

"Oh, we can leave that to the farmer," his companion remarked casually.

When the ride was over, Washington went back and carefully replaced the stones.

"Oh, General," said one of his companions, "you are too big a man to do that."

"On the contrary," replied Washington, "I am just the right size!"

"I AM getting on with my little book," wrote a lady approaching middle-age on 6th December 1876. The "little book" had been milling around her mind since 1871 when she had begun to take an interest in the welfare of the cab-horses she watched from her window.

Her name was Anna Sewell, and the book she was writing was "Black Beauty", which, when it was published, was judged as being "quite a nice story, but unlikely to have a large circulation".

How wrong that critic was! "Black Beauty" is still a children's favourite, selling steadily in many countries of the world.

Anna had no thought of fame when she wrote the book. She just wanted to tell the story of two horses, and some of the dreadful things that happened to them, as a plea for greater kindness to animals. It worked, too, for as a result of "Black Beauty" much of the cruel treatment of horses at that time was stamped out.

L

THE FRIENDSHIP BOOK

I CAN'T remember where I read "An optimist is as often wrong as the pessimist, but he is far happier."

It reminded me of a story I heard about Michelangelo. One day he was chipping away at a shapeless piece of rock when a passer-by asked what he was doing.

"I am releasing the angel that is imprisoned in this piece of marble," he replied.

DAVID DOUGLAS, a gardener's boy from Perthshire, became one of the greatest collectors of plants and trees. The magnificent Douglas Fir bears his name, and the flowering currant which brightens the days of early Spring was brought across the Atlantic by him.

He suffered great hardships as he searched the peaks and valleys of the Rocky Mountains for new treasures, though in his journal he made light of his troubles.

At one camp he and his guide were left with nothing to drink and not even a cup or mug. His guide pointed to the nearby stream and said simply, "This is my barrel and it is always running."

Often on a hot Summer day, when I am pouring a glass of water for myself, I picture Douglas drinking from the lonely stream and I realise once again how dependent we all are on the simple gifts of Nature.

BE not ignorant of any thing in a great matter or a small.   Ecclesiasticus 5:15

THE FRIENDSHIP BOOK

I AM sure that there are times when all of us, faced with someone in great trouble, feel that we just don't know what to say to them. When I have felt like this I have found great help in a story told about Thomas Carlyle and his friend, James Anthony Froude, the historian.

When Jane, Carlyle's wife, died, Froude went to see his friend. He sat down, could not say a word, stayed an hour and went away. Next day Thomas Carlyle wrote a letter to Froude thanking him for his sympathetic and understanding visit.

Truly an example of the saying, "Speech is silvern, but silence is golden" — words which Carlyle himself had quoted from the Swiss in one of his own books, "Sartor Resartus".

"DOWN your Way" is one of our most popular radio programmes. It started in 1946 and has visited hundreds of towns and villages, interviewing a variety of people with interesting things to say.

Its presenters have included Richard Dimbleby and Franklin Engelmann, but it was something said by Brian Johnston, who took over in 1972, which impressed me.

He wrote, "It's a lovely programme to do, because we are non-knockers. We go to a place to find out the *nice* things about it. The papers these days are full of stories about criminals and vandals, and of how selfish and uncaring our society has become, but if you were to come with us on our journeys round the country for 'Down your Way', you would be pleasantly surprised to find how many people are doing things to help other people."

GOOD COMPANIONS

Not in hours of earnest talk
  Does friendship seem to flourish,
But quiet ways and quiet days
  Leave memories to cherish.

THE FRIENDSHIP BOOK

J. M. ROBERTSON sent me this amusing poem entitled "Intrigue":

How am I going to tell her —
  My unsuspecting wife,
That now there is another
  Woman in my life?

Although I'm so much older,
  I shun each busy tongue
That dwells on my attachment
  For anyone so young.

Perhaps I'm being silly,
  And yet I can't deny
A triangle with a difference
  Is here, and glad am I.

Before you start condemning
  My conduct as quite mean,
May I say the other lady
  Is my little grand-child, Jean!

SIR ALEXANDER FLEMING, the discoverer of penicillin, once said that great advances in science were made less by outstanding knowledge and skill than by very careful observation.

Our own powers of observation may not lead to any world-shattering discovery, but they can certainly lead to a good deal of happiness as we see things others may not notice. Sir James Barrie once said of his fellow-writer, Thomas Hardy, "That man couldn't look out of a window without seeing something that he had never seen before."

THE FRIENDSHIP BOOK

MANY of us have found that constantly repeating some simple formula of positive, hopeful words, particularly last thing at night, can do a great deal towards developing confidence and an optimistic outlook on life.

A friend, whose life has been far from easy, tells me that his own outlook has been completely transformed by repeating confidently each night before he falls asleep, " Things will be better tomorrow!"

And what's more, he tells me they always are.

IN 1862 Osgood Mackenzie built his home on a bleak peninsula by Loch Ewe on the north-west coast of Scotland. He could have left the surroundings as they were, but instead, he started to create a garden overlooking the loch. The land was barren and before he could begin planting, tons of good earth had to be transported there. Today the Inverewe Gardens are famous, and many rare and tender plants from all over the world flourish there, warmed by the Gulf Stream.

Mackenzie's vision created a place of peace and delight which attracts visitors all the year round, for there is always something different to admire.

So many people can see only the gloomy side of life. If only there were more like Osgood Mackenzie who saw the potential of his own situation — and sought to make something of it.

AND he saith unto them, Follow me, and I will make you fishers of men.   Matthew 4:19

THE FRIENDSHIP BOOK

I INVITE you to join with me in a Love Game. That's puzzled you! Well, it's simply this — I've realised how difficult it is for some folk to say aloud, "I love you". We're all a bit reticent at times, aren't we? So often, in their own way, people act out their love, and we have to watch for it . . .

I began looking, and, believe me, I didn't have long to wait — the little girl down the road is having simple cookery lessons at school, and on the kitchen table today appeared four small cakes, with a tiny note, "With love from Claire XXX".

I went into the garden intending to finish the lawn-cutting from which I'd been called away earlier — and found my neighbour completing the job. "All done," he smiled.

Later in the day I called on some friends. They'd been making marmalade. "Here, have a jar," they said. "We made some extra for you."

Yes, love comes in such varying packages, and it's really quite exhilarating playing the Love Game. Try it!

PERHAPS you would not expect to find any wise counsel in a book written about fishing. If so, then you have never read Isaac Walton's "The Compleat Angler", which first appeared in 1653.

Among his many gems of wisdom is this one: "And cherish patience all your days. The angler will meet with a multitude of unexpected difficulties, but will keep smiling in spite of delays and heartbreaking disappointments, and will enjoy the unspeakable rapture of the fisherman's triumph at last."

It applies not only to angling but to life itself.

THE FRIENDSHIP BOOK

THE Lady of the House and I recently entertained a retired minister. He reflected on his retirement, and spoke of the friends he had made, his four children, three of them now married with families of their own, and how his grandchildren kept him so busy he seldom seemed to have much time for himself. "Take my advice," he smiled. "If you want a quiet retirement — don't make any friends or have any grandchildren. But it's far better if you do!"

A HUNDRED years ago this month, a book was published that eventually sold over a million copies and was translated into many languages. "Little Lord Fauntleroy" first appeared as a serial in an American children's magazine in November, 1885.

Its author Frances Hodgson Burnett, was born on 26th November 1849 in Manchester, where her father had an ironmonger's and silversmith's business. After his death the family moved to another part of the city and eventually Frances went to Canada.

It was in Canada and America that she became famous as a writer, but she never forgot Britain where her books also became very popular and she often came to stay in this country. In 1898 she leased Maytham Hall at Rolvenden in Kent, and it was here she first thought of the idea for her book, "The Secret Garden".

Her motto was "kindness to others" and although she did not always manage to live up to it as she desired, she was always eager to help people in distress, particularly in the village of Rolvenden which she loved. There she tried hard to live out her motto, and who can do better than that?

THE FRIENDSHIP BOOK

"I TOOK it all very philosophically." With these words an acquaintance of mine ended a long recital of a series of disasters that had befallen him on holiday. It prompted me to ask myself what we mean by "taking things philosophically".

My dictionary says that a philosopher is one who "seeks wisdom and knowledge". Does he therefore take things wisely and does knowledge breed a cheerful spirit?

It was a contented man who once said, "I have tried in my time to be a philosopher, but I don't know how; cheerfulness always breaks in."

For philosophers and non-philosophers alike, "letting cheerfulness break in" gets us through many a difficult time.

I WONDER if you live in one of the areas affected by boundary changes some years ago? I like the story of a group of Yorkshire villagers who were being interviewed at the time by a local newspaper journalist about the proposal to take part of the Bowland area where they lived into Lancashire.

Most of them argued their case vigorously but one would only keep repeating, "I'm agin it!" When at last he was persuaded to give a reason for his opposition to the scheme which would take him into Lancashire, he muttered, "I couldn't stand t'weather!"

OWE no man anything, but to love one another: for he that loveth another hath fulfilled the law.

Romans 13:8

THE FRIENDSHIP BOOK

IN a small Scottish market town I know, the rules are sometimes bent a little — and none the worse for that perhaps.

I'm thinking of a police sergeant who happened to notice a farmer getting into his car, parked where it shouldn't have been, on double yellow lines.

He waited till the farmer was in the car, then tapped on the window.

"Aye, Walter," he said, "isn't it a good thing they put down those double yellow lines or you wouldn't know where to park!"

Perhaps the policeman should have taken sterner action, but in a small town, strong-arm action isn't always the best way of working.

A MAN sat in his London home writing a letter to his young son in the year 1907. It was not an ordinary letter, nor did it give a load of instructions and advice on "how to be a good boy." It began simply, "Have you heard about the Toad?"

Kenneth Grahame, author of "The Wind in the Willows" and Secretary of the Bank of England was writing to his son Alastair.

It was his custom to tell Alastair bed-time stories. Many of these were tales of the little animals by the riverside at Cookham Dene, or along rivers in Cornwall. They were usually about the adventures of Mole, Ratty and Mr Badger.

The letters continued until the autumn of 1907 and were so enjoyed by Alastair that his father decided to make them into a book. "The Wind in the Willows" which appeared in October, 1908, became a children's favourite and has remained so ever since.

THE FRIENDSHIP BOOK

THE Lady of the House seemed somewhat put out when she related how she'd been waiting behind a man in the butcher's.

"What's your steak like?" he asked.

"It's as tender as a woman's heart," grinned the butcher, placing a piece on the block.

"Really?" said the customer. "Then I'll have a pound of sausages!"

REFLECTING on his career when he was nearly 90, the ex-Prime Minister, Harold Macmillan, was asked in a television interview about his reaction to the criticism which seems unavoidable in political life.

"Ah, well," he said, "in public life one tends on the one hand to be over-blamed, or on the other to be over-praised, and one has just to come to terms with these things."

A wise philosophy for all of us, whether in public life or not.

ISN'T it a pity that sometimes what ought to be a friendly conversation turns acrimonious? I believe wholeheartedly in the old saying, "It is better to lose an argument than to lose a friend."

That just "being right" isn't the most important thing in the world is well-illustrated by this humorous epitaph:

Here lies the body of Samuel Jay
Who died defending his right-of-way.
He was right, dead right, as he drove along,
But he's just as dead as if he'd been wrong.

SATURDAY—OCTOBER 29.

I HAD arranged to meet my friend Harry and go for a long walk. We left the car at a spot in the country and walked and chatted for three splendid hours.

Sometimes the clouds rolled up and then blew away. Once there was just a spot of rain. But it was a lovely walk and I said to Harry as we drove home, "Well, I never expected a day like that after looking at the awful weather forecast on TV last night."

"Oh, I never saw it," said Harry. "If I had, I would have put off the walk!"

I don't know what that proved, except that some folk have complete faith in the weathermen and some of us are willing to take a chance that the bad weather may come later than expected, or sometimes may not come at all.

As for me, I'm one of the take-a-chance brigade.

SUNDAY—OCTOBER 30.

WHOSOEVER shall compel thee to go a mile, go with him twain.   Matthew 5:41

MONDAY—OCTOBER 31.

ALL over the country tonight children will be having fun with their Hallowe'en turnip lanterns. Did you know that, years ago, people used to hang the lanterns on their gateposts to frighten away evil spirits?

It was a night of fear then, but happily the old superstitious beliefs no longer have any hold over us.

A lot of fears are imaginary, just like the old superstitions of the ancient Hallowe'en. Let's learn to laugh at those fears, too — in fact, to turn our fears into fun.

NOVEMBER

TUESDAY—NOVEMBER 1.

A YOUNG architect was admiring the soaring grace of Canterbury Cathedral. He said to his companion, a much older man:

"How did they manage to put up a building like this all those centuries ago? They had no big cranes; everything had to be done by hand. We couldn't do today what they did. What was their secret?"

"I can't tell you about that," said the other. "But I have heard it said that, in those days, men had convictions. Today, perhaps too many just have opinions."

WEDNESDAY—NOVEMBER 2.

A T the turn of the century, there was a man living in a Staffordshire village who had the reputation of being a bit simple. One day, as he was fishing in the lake, he saw the water bailiff approaching. Quickly he removed his bait and substituted an onion.

"Well, Jim, fishing are you?" said the bailiff. "Let's have a look at your bait."

On being shown the onion, the bailiff allowed him to continue, believing there was no danger that he would catch any fish.

That evening the two men met again in the village inn where Jim was showing his friends several fine trout.

"You never caught all those with an onion, Jim!" said the puzzled bailiff.

"Oh, no," said Jim. "You're the only one I caught with an onion!"

THE FRIENDSHIP BOOK

IN a television interview recorded shortly before her death, the actress Dame Flora Robson said that religion had always been a very important element in her life. Then she added, "But I always remember a piece of advice given to me long ago: 'Ask God's blessing on your work, but don't expect him to do it for you.'"

A new way of putting the old practical saying, "God helps those who help themselves."

IN cold, dark, winter days how we long for the sunshine! But can we have too much sunshine I wonder?

In his book "Second Skin", the writer and broadcaster, Edward Blishen says, "I remember, absurdly, my sensation in the tropics after days of this endless sunshine, longing for the daily uncertainties of the Northern sky".

Isn't it true that we can "have too much of a good thing"? There is an old legend of people who died and went to what was called "The Land of Everlasting Happiness", where there was no pain or discomfort of any kind. The flowers never faded. The sun never set. After a few hundred years of this, they began to get a bit bored, and, the story continues, when a quack doctor appeared on the scene selling pills which made people feel ill and their hair turn grey, he did a roaring trade!

Only a story, of course, but isn't this really just what Edward Blishen was talking about? It's often the darker things of life which make us more appreciative of the brighter things, our burdens which lead us to count our blessings.

THE FRIENDSHIP BOOK

OLD Mr Brown was housebound, but his two neighbours, Mrs Jones and Mrs Carr, made sure they visited him every day.

Mrs Jones always took him some of her home baking and while she was there she busied herself with odd jobs and tidied his room.

Mrs Carr, on the other hand, much to Mrs Jones's disgust, never took him anything or did any jobs. She just sat and talked to him, telling him all the local chit-chat and listening to his reminiscences.

Yet Mr Brown was equally grateful to both his visitors.

It is so easy to forget, like Mrs Jones, that not all our needs are purely practical ones. Like Martha and Mary, we may have different gifts to offer, but if we give them gladly, they are equally worthy.

FOR the kingdom of God is not in word, but in power.
                                        I Corinthians 4:20

IT'S not often I see my bank manager, but when I went into his office the other day, I found he was something of a philosopher. On his desk was a card bearing the following words:

> *Yesterday is a cancelled cheque.*
> *Tomorrow is a promissory note.*
> *Today is ready cash. Use it!*

I think that did me more good than a loan would have done!

ON THE CANAL

L

THE FRIENDSHIP BOOK

YOUNG Jonathan had got a nasty cut and needed to go to the hospital to have it attended. As he sat in the waiting room he noticed that the other children looked very worried as they went into the treatment room, but that they came out with a smile.

When Jonathan's turn came, he, too, went in looking anxious. After his wound had been cleaned and bandaged, the nurse called him over, told him he was a good boy and gave him a big hug. Need I tell you that Jonathan also left with a big smile on his face?

I am reminded of something Mother Teresa said about her work in Calcutta: "We can do no great things — only small things with great love."

HILDA TILNEY of Teignmouth sent me a copy of her little book of poetry, "Reflections". There are some lovely poems in it, but the one I want to share with you is this amusing confession of a romantic encounter!

I blew a kiss to a man tonight,
He smiled and winked at me;
His cheery face was round and bright,
He was a joy to see.

He filled my garden full of gold,
And said, "I'll grant a boon;
If you love me you'll ne'er grow old!"
The saucy man in the Moon!

I blew a kiss to a man tonight,
He said, "I'll never tell,"
And as my husband is in sight,
Perhaps it's just as well!

M

THE FRIENDSHIP BOOK

THE nightingale sings both day and night and its lovely liquid tone is a delight to all bird lovers.

There is a lovely story that the purity of its song was a gift from Mary, the mother of Jesus. When Mary was sitting nursing her baby, she sang quietly to lull him to sleep. A nightingale sitting nearby was so enchanted with the sweet music that it flew into the house and perched on Mary's shoulder, joining in her song.

When the baby Jesus had fallen asleep, Mary turned to the nightingale to thank it. "In recognition of your help," she said, "you shall have my voice, and for ever more people will stop and listen to its beauty."

A LITTLE while ago, the Lady of the House and I took a trip across the English Channel where we visited a British military cemetery.

It was a moving experience, and as we came away, I was reminded of these lines:

We came across a gravestone white,
So stark in a lush, foreign field,
In memory of an unknown lad
Who fell that our wounds might be healed.

No name was scribed upon that stone —
Just these poignant words from the strife:
"The greatest sacrifice of all —
The gift of an unfinished life".

I will reflect on these verses again this Remembrance Sunday when we think of the countless "unfinished lives".

THE FRIENDSHIP BOOK

AS I walked through my garden on a cold November day, I noticed that the winter jasmine climbing up the garage wall was already coming into flower. Soon there would be a cascade of bright yellow flowers to brighten the view from the kitchen window.

It seems strange that such spring-like flowers should begin to bloom in the darkest of months when most plants are resting. They seem to bring a ray of hope at a time when the days are at their shortest and dullest.

I was reminded of something I read recently: "Even in darkness, light dawns for those who believe."

It's something positive for us to hold on to and take comfort in — the light that always shines at the end of the tunnel.

AND some there be, which have no memorial; who are perished, as though they had never been. Their bodies are buried in peace; but their name liveth for evermore.   Ecclesiasticus 44;9, 44:14

I HAVE just been reading the autobiography of Fred Dibnah, the steeplejack who became a television personality. He writes about the dangers of working on high chimneys, but says he always works within adequate safety margins and takes no risks.

"Indeed," he says, "I have only once fallen off a ladder and that was a set of steps at home when I was decorating the kitchen!"

It's the little things of life which sometimes require the most attention.

THE FRIENDSHIP BOOK

TUESDAY—NOVEMBER 15.

THE Lady of the House and I had been discussing how often Murphy's Law works out in life. As you may remember, this says that anything that can go wrong will go wrong. For instance, if you drop a piece of jammy bread it will always land with the jammy side down.

A friend's little girl, Dawn, had been listening closely, then made a suggestion: "Don't you think it would have been better if whoever had the piece of bread had put the jam on the other side? Then the jammy side wouldn't have landed on the floor, would it, Mr Gay?"

Just try working that one out!

WEDNESDAY—NOVEMBER 16.

MOST people have heard of Toc H — the society aimed at Christian fellowship and social service which was founded in 1915 by an Army Chaplain, Rev. P. B. ("Tubby") Clayton. It takes its unusual name from Talbot House ("toc" being the signaller's "T".) a soldiers' social club in Flanders.

It was named after Gilbert Talbot (youngest son of the then Bishop of Winchester), a young man of great promise who was killed in the very early days of the war.

"Tubby" Clayton made more than a club of it — "a real home from home" many of the soldiers called it, and it was permeated by his own courage, cheerfulness and friendliness amid circumstances of great strain and danger, at a time when hundreds were being killed every day.

I think the message of Toc H has a message for us all — "Service is the rent we pay for our room on earth."

THE FRIENDSHIP BOOK

THE late Dag Hammarskjold, Swedish-born Secretary-General of the United Nations, was famous not only for his wise and patient leadership of that organisation, but also for his gift of putting great and wise thoughts into brief, pointed sayings.

One which no doubt helped him in his demanding work but could also guide us all in the ordinary undertakings of life was, "Never look down to test the ground before taking your next step: only he who keeps his eye fixed on the far horizon will find the right road."

NEXT time you are tempted to complain about the weather, think for a moment about these lines written by Barbara Jemison:

> *Don't fret about the weather,*
>   *My mother always said,*
> *For there are those oppressed by*
>   *pain*
>   *Who are confined to bed*
> *With no hope for the future,*
>   *Prisoners of ill-health,*
> *To whom all kinds of weather*
>   *Would bring the greatest wealth.*
> *To face a wild North-easter,*
>   *To trample through the snow,*
> *To feel the sting of hailstones*
>   *Would set their cheeks aglow.*
> *You'd never hear from their lips*
>   *Such things as we would say,*
> *Like "fed up with this weather"*
>   *Or "It's cold again today."*

THE FRIENDSHIP BOOK

THE courage and determination of the legless air-man, Sir Douglas Bader, won the admiration of millions of people. His greatness was enhanced by yet another quality. At a memorial service in London shortly after his death, Group Captain Cheshire said, " To me Douglas was, above everything else, a great encourager of his fellow men."

He who could so easily have given in to despair, became himself an inspiration to others.

WHEN I was a child, I spake as a child, I understood as a child, I thought as a child; but when I became a man, I put away childish things.

I Corinthians 13:11

THE hands of the clock do a lot more than just tell the time. All men and women who have served in the Armed Forces or even played golf, know exactly what is meant when told "It's at one o'clock", which means you should look just very slightly to the right of where you're standing.

Not long ago, I learned of a new use for the hands of the clock when a friend from Australia made an unexpected visit. We were talking of old acquaintances.

"Tom Hughes," said my friend. "Now, there's a real six o'clock man for you!"

"Six o'clock?" I asked.

My friend explained. "Yes. Like the hands at six o'clock, straight up and down. Dead straight. That's Tom Hughes."

THE FRIENDSHIP BOOK

LILY PARKER was born in 1900, so you know how many years her saintly face has been spreading sunshine around.

Some time ago she was travelling by train to Birmingham. At one station an elderly gentleman and a middle-aged lady got in — father and daughter, as it transpired. The father smiled, but he was very deaf and just sat there quietly. His daughter and Lily, however, quickly struck up a cheerful conversation, and soon discovered that they were both active members of their churches.

When the couple reached their destination and picked up their luggage to leave the carriage, the old gentleman leant across to Lily. Despite his deafness, he had evidently picked up enough of the conversation to realise one important thing.

He smiled at Lily and said quietly, "Your Father is my Father."

Isn't it wonderful how complete strangers can meet and find that they have so much in common, because they belong to the same divine family.

DURING the Last War a civil servant, looking through some documents, came across a piece of paper with some strange writing on it. He took it to be some sort of code and wondered if he had stumbled on secret enemy information, but before he could take it to the de-coding department it was snatched from him by a girl in the office who exclaimed, "I've been looking everywhere for that! It's my knitting pattern!"

A silly mistake? Maybe, but when I glance at the knitting books which the Lady of the House uses I can quite understand how he made it!

THE FRIENDSHIP BOOK

SIR JOSEPH BANKS was one of the early directors of the wonderful garden at Kew in London. His collectors travelled the world in search of the beautiful and the exotic.

When a new plant had flowered at Kew, Banks kept it for a year. Then he gave seedlings to those he knew would prize them and tend them well.

Generosity? Yes, but Banks, like all gardeners, knew that disaster might strike one of his treasures. If it was also growing in other gardens, all was not lost.

There's a saying about casting our bread upon the waters. Sir Joseph knew, as many people today in all walks of life know, just what that means.

"VISITING" is the title of this poem sent to me by Greta Aspland of Crawley in Sussex:

> Our stately homes I much admire;
> Such treasures they contain,
> That just one visit can't suffice,
> So I return again
> To view the antique furniture
> And crystal chandelier,
> Ancestral portraits in the hall,
> Great paintings by Vermeer;
> A music room of white and gold,
> With lute and harpsichord
> That conjure up a time long passed,
> When lady danced with lord . . .
> Quite soon it's time to leave once more
> And though it's been so fine,
> I'm glad my cottage waits for me,
> With treasures that are mine.

COUNTRY STROLL

SATURDAY—NOVEMBER 26.

TOMORROW is "Stir-up Sunday", the Sunday before Advent, and it is so called because in the Book of Common Prayer the collect for that day begins "Stir up, we beseech Thee, O Lord, the wills of thy faithful people."

As housewives heard this prayer in church, it was a reminder that if they had not already made their Christmas puddings, then they should make haste.

When pudding-making day arrived, the children liked to gather round the kitchen table and watch all the ingredients being mixed in a large bowl. Then they all gave it a stir and made a wish.

Schoolboys had their own interpretation of the collect for it reminded them that plum pudding was not far away and they used to run home together chanting,

> Stir up we beseech thee,
> The pudding in the pot,
> And when we get home
> We'll eat it all hot.

SUNDAY—NOVEMBER 27.

FOR as in Adam all die, even so in Christ shall all be made alive.   I Corinthians 15:22

MONDAY—NOVEMBER 28.

YOUNG Billy has been up to his riddles again. "Do you know why the man took a pencil to bed, Mr Gay?" he asked me the other day.

When I admitted I didn't know, he said, "To draw the curtains." Then he added, before he ran off, "I would tell you another joke about a pencil, but it hasn't any point!"

THE FRIENDSHIP BOOK

I WAS talking with a minister the other day about a couple whose marriage had just broken up.

I told him I couldn't understand it. "I had no idea there was anything wrong. Their house was always so beautiful," I said.

The minister looked at me. "When I visit a house that is *too* perfect, I hear a little warning bell ringing." He explained that it is often a sign that all is not well in the household.

In his experience, the over-perfection can mean that too much care is being lavished on the state of the house, and not enough on the life that should be going on inside it. Either that, or, sadder still, it is a sign that love has already fled that home, and the family is seeking compensation for the emptiness left behind.

LATE in 1953, a 21-year-old Londoner was looking forward to the appearance of his first book, and was most dismayed when his publisher told him it would not be issued until January 1954. He would miss the Christmas sales, and he feared his book wouldn't be noticed. Deeply despondent about it he tried to have the date changed.

His wise old publisher, however, told him that in a month like January, any book more than ordinarily interesting would be assured of good reviews, and its popularity would be guaranteed. And he was right, for when the first novel by the then unknown Kingsley Amis was published in the early days of 1954, "Lucky Jim" was an immediate success. It established its author's reputation as a highly perceptive writer of social comedy.

Sometimes it pays to wait.

DECEMBER

THURSDAY—DECEMBER 1.

THE Chinese, I am told, have a story about a court official who was ordered by the emperor to travel round the country and discover the best methods of improving his subjects.

He reported that he had spent much time reading gravestone inscriptions extolling those who had passed on. It was a pity, he remarked, that it was not possible to dispose of the emperor's present subjects and restore to life those who had gone and were obviously so much better.

It's only a story, but it made me think how many people would love a word of encouragement NOW instead of having their good deeds remembered when they have gone.

> *If you can give a word of praise*
> *And downcast spirits help to raise,*
> *Now's the time.*
> *If kindly deeds you do remark,*
> *Don't keep your feelings in the dark,*
> *But praise them now!*

FRIDAY—DECEMBER 2.

WHAT a lot of sayings there are connected with various parts of the human body, such as "put your best foot forward", "lend a hand", "nose to the grindstone", "don't lose your head" and so on.

But here's one I came across only recently. I think it has a lot of wisdom in it: "There's only a slight difference between keeping your chin up and sticking your neck out, but it's worth knowing."

It is, indeed!

THE FRIENDSHIP BOOK

MRS THOMPSETT, a woman well into her 90's, has just moved into our neighbourhood to live with her grand-daughter, Rachael, and her great-grandchildren.

"Where do you want to go first, then, Gran?" asked Rachael, as Mrs Thompsett was settling in. "To the surgery to register with our family doctor, in case you're ill?"

"Certainly not!" was the rapid retort. "I have to go straight to the Town Hall."

"But why?" asked her surprised grand-daughter.

"I want to make sure my name goes on the register of electors — I don't want to miss my chance of voting at the next election!"

First things first!

DRAW nigh to God, and he will draw nigh to you.   James 4:8

SIR NEVILLE CARDUS, the music critic and cricket writer, was once asked how he explained his twin passion for these two very different subjects. He replied, "Well, they have this in common—they both have slow movements!"

I fancy that if cricket and music consisted of nothing but "slow movements" the thrill and excitement would soon go out of them, but certainly they do have their place.

It's a good thing, too, that life has its "slow movements"—times of relaxation, stillness and peace. What would we do without them?

THE FRIENDSHIP BOOK

TUESDAY—DECEMBER 6.

THE famous painter, J. M. W. Turner, had many of his pictures hung in the Royal Academy. He also served on the Hanging Committee which made the final decision as to which pictures should be shown at the annual exhibition.

On one occasion he was disappointed to find that a picture he had particularly admired was among those left out.

"I really feel it ought to be shown," he said to his fellow-selectors.

"Who is it by?" asked one of the others, looking at the label. "Never heard of him," he grunted when he saw the name of an unknown artist. "Anyhow, we've made our decision now. There's no more room."

"Oh, yes, there is," said Turner and moving across, he took down a painting of his own and put that of the unknown artist in its place.

WEDNESDAY—DECEMBER 7.

AS the Lady of the House and I were sitting over a 'cuppa' one afternoon, we began to consider how many people are involved in our lives whenever we do the simplest thing. Take that tea, for example. We had needed water and heat, both of which required work by others. The tea itself came to us thanks to tea-planters, pickers, packers and shippers. Then there was the paper for wrapping it, and the shopkeeper from whom we bought it, the cups we drank it from, and the milk and sugar — my list could be a great deal longer.

It is good sometimes to spare a thought, not only for our friends who mean so much to us, but for all the people whose lives touch ours in such a variety of ways.

THE FRIENDSHIP BOOK

I HAVE read many a tribute by a famous man to his wife, but this one, by Sir Alec Guinness, who has given so much pleasure in films and on TV, seems to me to be rather different. He writes in his autobiography:

"I cannot imagine what life would have been like had I never known her, or had not had the courage to suggest marriage. What sort of life would it be if I didn't have someone to grumble to about the missing coffee-pot, the burned potatoes, the paint on the door knob, or the forgotten arrival of my train from London?"

"Someone to grumble to . . ." He means sharing, doesn't he? Sharing the good and the bad, just like every couple do in the wonderful partnership of marriage.

WE all know the saying "mutton dressed as lamb" which is applied to someone who acts like a much younger person.

It's not the same thing at all as keeping young at heart.

George Stephen, who for many years during a long life was first citizen of Aberdeen, summed up his attitude to age in these lines:

> *The advancing years roll on*
> *And their flight we cannot stay,*
> *With the past forever gone,*
> *All its glories fled away.*
> *Yet this song of hope is sung—*
> *Writ in syllables of gold—*
> *"We'll succeed in keeping young*
> *For we're willing to grow old!"*

THE FRIENDSHIP BOOK

READERS of Charles Dickens's "Nicholas Nickleby" will be familiar with the business partners, the Cheeryble brothers, Ned and Charles, who were so good to Nicholas and always ready to give generously to every good cause. There was no reluctant giving on their part.

"How very kind of you to give us the privilege of helping!" they would say.

Too good to be true? Not at all. Dickens modelled these characters on two brothers named Grant who ran a large business in Manchester. Born in poverty, they had built up a prosperous business through hard work and integrity.

However, they never forgot their early days and they delighted in helping others in similar circumstances. They were the sort of givers whom the Bible says God loves — "Cheerful givers". Dickens certainly gave them the right name!

EVERY good gift and every perfect gift is from above.   James 1:17

THIS little verse is titled "Singing", although it's not just about the art of song, but about how we live our lives:

> We must write the song
> Whatever the words,
> Whatever its rhyme or metre;
> And if it is sad, we must make it glad,
> And if sweet, we must make it sweeter.

M

TO HIS GLORY

THE FRIENDSHIP BOOK

A FRIEND of ours has to go abroad a good deal on business, but is not very keen on travel. He says, "I never look forward to going, and I can't say I really enjoy myself when I'm there, but looking back I'm always glad I went!"

Well, that's something, I suppose, but what a lot he misses! Two thirds of the enjoyment of life, in fact. For surely there is great joy in looking forward to something, in entering fully into it while it lasts, and in being able to look back upon it with gladness and gratitude.

"IT is from the struggle, not the victory, that we gain strength. Not what I am, but what I strove to be, that comforts me."

These words are from Jerome K. Jerome's autobiography. Jerome was born at Walsall, Staffordshire, on 2nd May 1859. He was only 12 when his father died, and two years later he took a job as a railway clerk. Out of his £26 annual salary he helped to maintain his mother and sister.

After his mother's death, life became even more difficult. He tried various jobs, being, in turn, a travelling actor, builder's clerk, schoolmaster and solicitor's clerk. However, he also became interested in writing and began to make a name for himself with humorous sketches. In 1889, publication of the comic masterpiece, "Three Men in a Boat", brought him fame and security. Other books and plays followed.

Remarkable, isn't it, that the man who suffered early hardships and financial worries went on to write some of the funniest and best-loved books in the English language?

THE FRIENDSHIP BOOK

IN the Nativity play at our local primary school, the parts of the three wise men were taken by little boys from the first year.

Presenting their gifts at the stable, the first said, "Gold"; the second said, "Myrrh"; and the third piped up, "And Frank sent this."

MOST people, if asked on the occasion of a Golden Wedding to what they attribute their happy life together, will have a ready answer. Recently I read this recipe which seems to combine all the main ingredients for happiness in family life and indeed in any relationship:

> 4 cups of Love
> 2 cups of Loyalty
> 3 cups of Forgiveness
> 1 cup of Friendship
> 1 cup of Understanding
> 2 spoons of Hope
> 2 spoons of Tenderness
> 4 quarts of Faith
> 1 barrel of Laughter

Take Love and Loyalty, mix thoroughly with Faith. Blend it with Tenderness, Kindness and Understanding. Add Friendship and Hope, sprinkle abundantly with Laughter. Bake it with Sunshine and serve daily in generous helpings.

What a lot of wisdom and commonsense there is to be found here! To apply just a fraction of it each day to the people close to us, could bring enormous benefits.

SATURDAY—DECEMBER 17.

I REMEMBER seeing a newspaper cartoon in which a wife was addressing Christmas cards, and saying to her husband, "We sent them one last year and they didn't send us one, so they probably won't send us one this year because they'll think we won't send them one because they didn't last year."

We can smile at that, but it's a pity if, at Christmas, or any other time, we are more concerned with receiving than with giving.

SUNDAY—DECEMBER 18.

SET your affection on things above, not on things on the earth. Colossians 3:2

MONDAY—DECEMBER 19.

THE poet Elsie S. Campbell wrote these lovely verses which so movingly describe how two people "grow together" with the passing years:

> Years of togetherness
>   We two have known;
> Sweet depths of happiness
>   Strangely our own.
>
> Silence between us now
>   Tranquilly flows;
> Words may be scarce and few,
>   Each surely knows . . .
>
> This world's most precious bliss
>   Now and forever
> Lies but in simply this:
>   "Being together."

CHRISTMAS THOUGHTS

TUESDAY—DECEMBER 20.

THIS is the time of year when millions of children address their letters to Santa Claus with their Christmas requests.

One small boy asked his mother what address he should put on his note. "Oh, just 'Santa Claus' will find him," she said.

But the lad was not satisfied with this, and after thinking for a moment or two he wrote, "Santa Claus, North Pole, Near God."

I think he was closer to the real meaning of Christmas than perhaps he realised.

WEDNESDAY—DECEMBER 21.

I DISCOVERED this lovely prayer by Robert Louis Stevenson quite recently: "The day returns and brings us the petty round of irritating concerns and duties. Help us to perform them with laughter and kind faces. Help us to play the man. Let cheerfulness abound with industry. Bring us to our resting beds weary and content and undishonoured; and grant us in the end the gift of sleep."

Stevenson has delighted many with his stirring adventure stories and yet they were written in the face of ill-health which dogged him from early childhood. He had to abandon the career he had hoped for in engineering and he endured great pain and approaching blindness.

Yet, at the height of his suffering, a friend was able to write, "In silence and the dark, he is still cheery and undaunted."

Until the end of his life, Stevenson was able to rise above his pain and to maintain the cheerful courage which his faith had given him. He was a great man indeed.

THE FRIENDSHIP BOOK

A FEW of us — all neighbours — were chatting over the garden fence. Will remarked that it was 20 years that day since they moved into their present house. That started us talking about landmarks in our lives. One man remembered how a chance meeting had led to a job that changed his life. And so it went on.

Then Andrew, who has just come to live near us and is recovering from a serious operation, chimed in:

"I had a landmark just last night. I'd had some stitches out yesterday and last night was the first night for six weeks I'd been able to sleep soundly lying on my side."

Yes, our landmarks come in all shapes!

I LIKE this delightful story about Joseph, Mary and the baby Jesus on their flight into Egypt.

As they travelled along, the night got cold and frosty and they stopped to rest in a cave. A little spider saw them arrive and, to keep them warm during the bitter night he spun a silken web across the entrance of the cave.

During the night some of Herod's soldiers came along searching for the baby boys which he had ordered to be killed. When they reached the cave they were about to go in when the captain noticed the web, still intact across the cave and covered with hoar frost.

He was sure that nobody could be inside or the web would have been torn, so he ordered the soldiers to leave it, and Jesus, Joseph and Mary slept on safely.

This is why, they say, we decorate our Christmas trees with tinsel, to remind us of the silvery web that protected the Holy Family from Herod's cruelty.

THE FRIENDSHIP BOOK

ON Christmas Eve, 1937, an Australian radio announcer, Norman Banks, was sitting at the window of his Melbourne flat when he heard music from the open window opposite. There he saw an old lady with a lighted candle in her hand listening to a carol.

This fired his imagination and the following Christmas, he held his first open-air Carols by Candlelight service — a custom which has since spread all over Australia. The Melbourne service, which has been held each year since, has been broadcast round the world, millions have shared in it, and thousands of pounds have been raised for charity, all because of that old lady with her candle.

AND when they were come into the house, they saw the young child with Mary his mother, and fell down, and worshipped him.   Matthew 2:11

THESE lines on "The Joy of Giving", were written by John Greenleaf Whittier:

Somehow not only for Christmas,
But all the long year through,
The joy that you give to others
Is the joy that comes back to you.

And the more you spend in blessing
The poor and lonely and sad,
The more of your heart's possessing
Returns to make you glad.

SERENITY

When the everyday world seems full of care,
Seek your haven; shelter there.

THE FRIENDSHIP BOOK

A FRIEND of the late Dr Albert Schweitzer arranged for a small group of people to meet him on a very brief stop at Cleveland during an American trip. They went to a restaurant near the station for breakfast at which the hostess had arranged for Schweitzer's favourite Alsatian coffee cake to be served at the end of the meal.

When that moment came, Schweitzer was handed the knife to do the honours. Glancing round the table, he counted nine people, but carefully cut ten slices.

"One for the young lady who has so graciously served us," he said, offering a portion to the waitress.

T HE comedian Tommy Trinder met George VI soon after he succeeded to the throne. They had met before and the King said, " Well, Trinder, you've done well since I saw you last."

Tommy stuck out his chin and replied, " You haven't done so badly yourself, sir!"

I WAS reading recently of an Arctic expedition. It told of the intense cold, the agonies of frostbite, the trackless wastes, the perils from icefloes, and much more besides. It seems to me that few situations demand greater courage.

Yet it was an Arctic explorer, Frederick Johnson, who said, "Worry does not empty tomorrow of its troubles — it empties today of its strength."

If *he* could say that, faced with the perils of the Arctic, I think we might find it helpful in our own "winters of discontent".

THE FRIENDSHIP BOOK

THE London poet Joyce Frances Carpenter sent me this thoughtful poem:

> *The year is past; what did we give?*
>> *What did you gain, and what regret?*
> *Was it a year you'd like to live*
>> *Right through again, or just forget?*
> *Were there mistakes? Did you cause pain?*
>> *Withhold your love from someone dear?*
> *Did all your efforts seem in vain*
>> *And every hope turn into fear?*
> *Remember you can start anew,*
>> *Resolve to live a better way,*
> *Forget past errors, sadness, too.*
>> *Tomorrow is another day!*

HERE'S a thought for the end of the year: "Mankind's greatest need is not to be informed but to be reminded."

Of course information and knowledge are important. Our minds ought to be ever receptive to new ideas — considering them, weighing them up and deciding what part they ought to play in our lives.

But we also have a lot to remember, a lot we're in danger of forgetting — the influences which have shaped our lives, the people who have helped us, the successes which have gladdened us and the failures which have taught us lessons we could have learned in no other way.

As the year closes, let's spend a little time *reminding* ourselves, doing, as it were, a bit of year-end mental stock-taking.

A happy New Year to you all!

Where the Photographs were taken

L'ETACQ, JERSEY — *Solitude.*

BETCHWORTH, SURREY — *No Hurry.*

LA CORBIERE, JERSEY — *Artistry.*

CONISTON WATER, LANCASHIRE — *Contemplation.*

CONISTON VILLAGE, LANCASHIRE — *Inspiration.*

GATEHOUSE OF FLEET, KIRKCUDBRIGHTSHIRE — *Ever New.*

KILCHURN CASTLE, ARGYLL — *Thrilling.*

WINDSOR CASTLE, BERKSHIRE — *Splendid Pageantry.*

PORTHMADOG, CARNARVONSHIRE — *Quiet Waters.*

GLEN SHIEL, ROSS AND CROMARTY — *Highland Tranquillity.*

NEWPORT-ON-TAY, FIFE — *Opposite Tuesday 24th May.*

RINGWOOD, HAMPSHIRE — *Summer's Glory.*

ST JOHN'S COLLEGE, CAMBRIDGE — *Opposite Sunday 26th June.*

BRAY, BERKSHIRE — *Village Idyll.*

ROYAL BOTANIC GARDENS, EDINBURGH — *Opposite Friday 29th July.*

CORN DU, PEN Y FAN, MONMOUTHSHIRE — *Achievement.*

SEILEBOST, HARRIS — *The Presence.*

ABERPORTH, CARDIGANSHIRE — *Regatta Day.*

SWAN GREEN, HAMPSHIRE — *Autumn Majesty.*

SALISBURY CATHEDRAL, WILTSHIRE — *By Avon.*

CUTMILL, SURREY — *Good Companions.*

WORSLEY, LANCASHIRE — *On The Canal.*

CHICHESTER CATHEDRAL, SUSSEX — *To His Glory.*

PLOCKTON, ROSS AND CROMARTY — *Serenity.*

Printed and Published by D. C. THOMSON & CO., LTD.,
185 Fleet Street, London EC4A 2HS.

© D. C. Thomson & Co., Ltd., 1988

ISBN 0 85116 407 2